HAPPY CAT HAPPY YOU

Quick Tips for Building a Bond with Your Feline Friend

ARDEN MOORE

Storey

The mission of Storey Publishing is to serve our customers by publishing practical information that encourages personal independence in harmony with the environment.

Edited by Lisa H. Hiley
Art direction by Alethea Morrison
Cover and book design by Jessica Hische
Indexed by Nancy D. Wood

Printed in the United States by R.R. Donnelley
10 9 8 7 6 5 4 3 2 1

Library of Congress Cataloging-in-Publication Data

Moore, Arden.
  Happy cat, happy you/Arden Moore.
    p. cm.
  Rev. ed. of: 50 simple ways to pamper your cat. c2000.
  Includes index.
  ISBN 978-1-60342-033-4 (pbk. : alk. paper)
  1. Cats. I. Moore, Arden. 50 simple ways to pamper your cat. II. Title.
SF447.M66 2008
636.8—dc22

2008022438

*To my fabulous felines, Callie and Murphy,
and to all the cats who deliver joy and
delight to our lives.*

ACKNOWLEDGMENTS

I extend full-throttle purrs of gratitude to all the veterinarians, animal behaviorists, and pet lovers who generously shared their ideas in this book to make this planet a much better place for our feline friends. Special thanks to my editor, Lisa Hiley, for bringing out the very best in these pages.

CONTENTS

Nothing signifies bliss better than a happy purr. Or being affectionately head-butted by your feline. Or having your empty lap quickly filled with a cat — or two — ready to cuddle. There's a reason why cats outnumber dogs in households, and it goes beyond not needing to be escorted to the nearest fire hydrant for bathroom breaks. Cats are cool. They're respectful. In their own dignified way, they enhance our lives. In facts, cats are proving to be the *purr-fect* prescription for good health.

Paw through these pages and you will discover hundreds of ways to celebrate that wonderful partnership you have with your feline pal. Learn how to take the ho-hum out of mealtime by bringing out the lion-like hunter in your tabby. Find out how a Ping-Pong ball in an empty bathtub can trigger the true jock inside your cat and why going a bit *fang shui* with your home décor can create harmony in your household. This book is filled with simple, easy tips designed to make life truly the cat's meow.

Count yourself fortunate to have a feline or more in your life — and your heart. I do every day.

Paws Up!

Arden Moore

Bringing Out the Feline Finest in Both of You

Chapter One

HAPPY CAT HAPPY YOU

THE ADAGE THAT DOG IS MAN'S BEST FRIEND BEGS CHALLENGING. I'LL TAKE THE SOUND OF A FULL-throttle purr over the thump of a wagging tail any day. Cats can bring out the best in you just as much as any dog — that's a medical fact. Studies show that interacting with your cat in a meaningful, nonrushed way can lower your blood pressure, reduce your stress, and help you to maintain a healthier outlook. Looks like cats are a purr-fect prescription, and that news is easy to swallow.

And what about the myth that cats are aloof? Nonsense. Cats crave human companionship — they just have too much dignity to cover you with kisses or worse, drool with delight. All cat lovers know how fantastically fortunate they are to share their lives with a fabulous feline!

THINGS WE CAN LEARN
from OUR CATS

. . . .

Cats live in the present, free of guilt and other ugly emotions. Think like your cat and try not to get caught up in "should haves" or "what ifs." Stop lamenting about the past and fretting about the future, and strive to live in the moment and take things as they come.

Cats value solitude. Most cats don't stick to you like Velcro every minute of the day. For many people, spending time alone is highly underrated, yet it is vital to recharge. Treat yourself to five minutes of solitude each day. If your cat wants to join you, that's fine, but no phones or other human distractions.

Cats are candid. They ask for what they want ("more tuna, please"). They can be quite persistent in pursuing their goal (such as that bug skittering across the floor). So if you want something, go for it! (Just be sure to keep your claws in.)

Book a date with your cat. I'm not talking about taking Max to the movies. We all know that most cats are not big fans of cars or leaving their home turf. Instead, make the effort to spend some quality time each day with your cat.

He deserves more than a quick greeting or a brief scratch on the head when you rush off to work or return home. Take a moment to pick up your pet for a purposeful cuddle whenever the opportunity presents itself.

TERRIFIC TIP

Use your cat's name every time you talk to her so that she recognizes it. Most cats will soon realize that their names are associated with good things, such as praise, petting, or treats.

Share your cat's funny antics and cool tricks with your pet-loving friends. It feels good to brag a bit, and with all the stress we face these days, people deserve to hear some upbeat news. Just remember: boasting should be a two-way street, so be a good listener when others wish to share a purr-fectly good tale about their own feline pal.

KEEP IT QUIET

. . . .

Cats hear at least six times better than we do, so whether you want to rock out to Bruce Springsteen or rap with Jay-Z or waltz to Lawrence Welk, respect your cat's sensitive ears and keep the volume at a moderate level or wear headphones.

GOING IN-CAT-NITO

....

If your cat is willing to play along with this, fit her with some fun sunglasses, a cute hat, or a bright bandana. Give her plenty of praise and a treat for complying. Social cats with a bit of diva in their characters may welcome accessories and will certainly appreciate being in the spotlight. (Accessorize during supervised playtimes only as a bandana and other items could choke her.)

Bring out your natural teaching abilities by showing a cat-loving child — perhaps a niece or nephew or neighbor — how to give a therapeutic massage or teach a simple trick to your kid-welcoming feline. My two cats, Callie and Murphy, are very patient around youngsters and serve as ideal feline role models.

I've taught kids between ages 8 and 12 how to get Callie to "work her abs" by leaping up to snare a treat with her paws and how to get Murphy to jump up on cue by having the child tap the chair. My cats like the treats and attention and the kids enjoy taking the role of leader. It's win-win for everyone!

CHATTY CAT

My first kitten, Corky, was nicknamed Loud Mouth — for good reason. He was a Siamese, a breed prone to vocalization. If your cat makes conversation, chat back. Sure, you may not be able to speak fluent feline, but your cat will appreciate your effort. My cat, Callie, answers me with "I-mean-now" vocals whenever I ask her if she would like a treat. She has trained me quite well!

THE CAT'S MEOW

. . . .

Cats are capable of making as many as 20 distinct sounds, each with a specific message. Unfortunately, no one has published a *Berlitz Guide to Cat Chat*, but here are some translation tips to prevent you from committing any feline faux pas.

Mew. These tiny sounds are made by young kittens, usually seeking food or warmth.

Chirp. This musical trilling sound seems to end in a question mark and usually means a friendly greeting, such as "welcome home."

Meow. Your cat is demanding your immediate attention. She may be declaring, "You're late with breakfast" or "Let's play — now."

Hiss. Plain and simple, this sinister sound means "back off."

Purr. No one really knows how they do it, but somehow cats manage to breathe while making noise with their mouths closed. Cats purr mostly when contented, but some also purr during stressful situations, such as during a vet visit.

IN *the* BLINK *of an* EYE

. . . .

While direct and prolonged eye contact feels threatening to cats, watch for this feline sign of affection and comfort when you catch your cat's eye: a relaxed "wink" of both eyes. Try blinking at her first to see if you can elicit a response. It's a silent and flattering way to "chat" with your cat.

When your cat rubs her cheek or body against you, she is marking you with special scent glands. It's her way of declaring to others, "Hey, this is *mine*." Don't worry; this isn't the same type of mark that cats make when they spray urine.

Only other animals can pick up this scent, though you might find visual evidence of it on the leg of a light-colored chair or the edge of a wall where your cat frequently marks. Over time, the oil from the glands can leave a residue (these smudges easily disappear with the use of a household multipurpose cleaner).

THE TAIL *of a* KITTY

. . . .

The tail is used for balance, and it also acts as a mood barometer. When it's held loosely upright while the cat is walking, it signals confidence. A tail that flicks toward you means "hello, my friend." Whipping the tail from side to side or thumping it on the floor signifies agitation. A lightly twitching tail conveys relaxed alertness. A puffed-up tail indicates total fright.

WHY WHISKERS?

· · · · · · · · · · · · · ·

The whiskers are used to detect space. Cats have 24 whiskers spaced in four rows on each side of the face. These sensitive organs protect the eyes and allow the cat to size up the width of entries. If the whiskers clear, the entire body can slither through.

Whiskers also act a bit like sonar and are able to "sense" a mouse in the dark house without even coming into contact with this trespassing rodent. As amazing as the whiskers are, the mouse does need to be within a couple of inches of them for the feline sonar system to activate.

The feline nose knows. When you witness your cat sniffing around the house, she is not just "stopping to smell the roses," especially if you have more than one cat or have recently had visitors (either human or animal). Each time a cat sniffs another cat's scent left on furniture or walls, she learns a mini-bio: the cat's gender, whether he is intact or neutered, his age, and his health status. Imagine if we could size up a person by taking a quick sniff!

Your cat's ability to pick up high-frequency sounds makes her better than any dog at detecting a mouse in the house. A cat's ears contain more than 40,000 nerve fibers, which allow cats to hear very high and very low frequencies. Only the horse and the porpoise have greater frequency ranges.

ONE CAT *or* TWO?

. . . .

Some cats love being the one and only feline in your household and your heart. If you want to know if your solo cat would welcome the addition of another cat to the house, watch how she reacts to other cats who she sees outside your home or those who may visit with house-guests. If your cat flees and hides or tries to fight with the other cat, she is probably best left as a solitary cat.

If you find that you can have only one cat in your home, you can always extend a caring paw to street cats. Check with local animal shelters and cat rescue groups to find out how you can help feed feral cats. These cats prefer living in colonies to being house cats but appreciate receiving nutritious meals on a regular basis.

TERRIFIC TIP

Don't yell at your cat when you catch her clawing your sofa. Instead, clap your hands or make a hissing noise to interrupt the unwanted behavior. Channel her need to scratch by providing sturdy scratching posts in various locations.

NO SWEET TOOTH

. . . .

Cats don't like sweets the way people do. That's probably because they have only 473 taste buds, compared with 9,000 on the human tongue. That's why they love stinky fish and strongly flavored meats so much. We may crave cookies and chocolates, but with our cats we should share bits of tuna instead (chocolate isn't good for them).

Need a reason to play with your cat? I'll dish out five:

- Prevent your feline from morphing into a hairy basketball from lack of exercise.

- Stave off feelings of anxiety in your cat that can result from too much time spent alone.

- Bolster your cat's trust and your bond with her.

- Eradicate boredom, which could lead to inappropriate behaviors such as climbing the curtains.

- Foster a feeling of confidence in your cat by honing his stalking and pouncing skills.

A BRIGHT IDEA

. . . .

Cats are the champions of power napping,
but Thomas Edison, a famous cat lover, was also
an advocate of power naps lasting no more than
20 minutes. Share his advice — and his affection
for felines — by treating yourself to an occasional
afternoon siesta with your cat. A short snooze
gives your body a chance to relax, recharge, and
revive. Persuading a cat to nap in the middle of
the afternoon is no problem; after all, the typical
tabby sleeps up to 18 hours a day.

MUST LOVE CATS

....

A Google search of the key words "tips for dating people with cats" yields more than 1.6 million hits. Welcome to the new world of dating — in which a cat or other pet may play a big part in your social life. Check out online dating services such as *www.datemypet.com* that cater to cat lovers. Seek companions who share your interest in felines by attending breed rescue events, cat shows, or fundraisers linked to local shelters.

Cats are creatures of routine. **They don't need to wear watches — they possess an uncanny knack for knowing when to wake you up, demand breakfast, and expect your return home from work. Nurture your cat's sense of security by establishing daily routines for playtime, feeding, and grooming.**

NOT *on MY* PILLOW, PLEASE

. . . .

Love your cat but not her habit of sleeping on your pillow at night? Try positioning a pillow similar to yours, with your scent on it, at the foot of your bed or in a cat bed in your bedroom. Keep moving her to the new spot until she learns that it is hers. Then both of you can enjoy a sound night's sleep. Talk about creature comforts!

If your cat hangs around when you're in the kitchen or bathroom and begs for a drink from the faucet, go ahead and indulge him. Most cats prefer water in motion to water in a bowl. Just remember to stop the drip when you exit to prevent getting socked with a huge water bill!

If you prefer a "no cats on counters" rule, try pouring water into a bowl on the floor, making sure it splashes a bit to catch kitty's interest. Better yet, provide your pal with his own little oasis by purchasing a special watering bowl that provides a continuous drip of fresh water.

CRAZY *for* CATNIP

One out of two cats craves catnip, the fragrant herb from the mint family. The plant's buds contain an essential oil called nepetalactone that evokes such feline antics as chin and cheek rubbing, rolling and kicking, and even leaping into the air.

Opt for organic catnip — it's the most potent — and always store this herb in an airtight container to keep it aromatic. Its effects last between 5 and 15 minutes for most cats.

NOT SO CRAZY *for* CATNIP

Some cats turn their noses up at catnip. No worries. Try honeysuckle-filled toys instead. Honeysuckle elicits a similar but less intense reaction than catnip for some cats. You must moisten the honeysuckle to activate its aroma in the hope of bringing out the play in your cat.

S-T-R-E-T-C-H

. . . .

Cats are born yoga teachers. **They seem to know that stretching reduces muscle tension and stiffness, improves blood and lymph circulation, and enhances flexibility and range of motion. Observe how your cat often performs a stretch ritual each morning before vacating your bed. She holds a stretch for a few seconds to maximize the health benefits.**

Mimic your cat by spending a full minute stretching out before you even get out of bed. Lie on your back with your legs extended and your arms above your head. Take a deep breath and slowly exhale as you stretch from head to toe. Think only about the stretch and how good it feels to your awakening muscles.

CALM DOWN!

. . . .

Embrace the power of petting. Scientists report that people who pet their cats experience an increase in theta waves, a brain wave pattern that shows a reduction in feelings of anxiety.

Petting your cat for just a few minutes releases a healthy amount of positive biochemicals, those "feel-good" hormones such as dopamine, oxytocin, prolactin, and serotonin. At the same time, levels of "fight or flight" biochemicals such as cortisol are reduced. Research shows that the good feelings work both ways, meaning that your cat benefits as well.

Therapeutic massage is a hot trend among cat lovers who realize the medical, bonding, and behavioral benefits of providing purposeful touch for their felines. Here are some tips for a marvelous massage:

- Approach your cat slowly and speak in a soothing tone.

- Let your cat pick the time and place.

- Use clean hands that are free of oils, creams, and lotions.

- Look for lumps, cuts, fleas, and ticks.

- Stroke toward the heart to enhance healthy blood flow.

- Pay attention to your cat's feedback signs. If he hangs around, gives you a sleepy glance, or even falls asleep, you've got the right touch. If he starts wiggling, resisting, and trying to escape, end the session.

- Enroll in a feline massage class. The best instructors are licensed massage therapists who have taken additional certification courses in cat massage.

Here's a variety of magic massage motions to try:

Circling. Move your fingers in small circles.

Flicking. Pretend that you are lightly brushing imaginary crumbs off of a table.

Gliding. Make flowing, continuous motions from head to tail with the palm of your hand or your fingers.

Kneading. Use your palm and all five fingers to gently caress the spinal area.

Rubbing. Move your fingers along your cat's body slowly, exerting varying pressure.

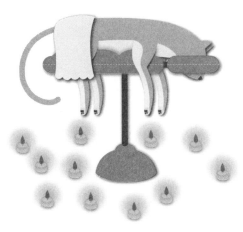

Splurge and hire a professional **pet photographer** for a photo session with you and your fabulous feline. Put the best images on the wall in frames or inside one of those nifty photo frames that feature a computer- ized slide show. Or cus- tomize your holiday cards and sign them with your cat's paw print. Your cat will welcome the added atten- tion she receives during this pose-and-click session.

TERRIFIC TIP

Toss the plastic top from a
soda pop bottle into the empty
bathtub for your cat to swat
around like a feline goalie.

BE KIND *to* ANISMALS WEEK

....

Celebrate this annual event (held during early May) by contacting your local animal shelter to see what events are being planned and how you may assist.

If you are a teacher or have children or grand-children, encourage them to write a story about being kind to cats and share it with their classmates.

Or treat a favorite senior citizen who loves cats by offering to take your social tabby over for regular visits. You give her the opportunity for a friendly fur fix without the responsibilities of owning and caring for a cat.

Cats are good at interpreting our body language and our intonations. They understand voice tone much better than specific words, so move calmly and speak quietly if you want your cat to cuddle up. Some savvy cats, however, do seem to know the word *treat* even when it's spelled out!

CATS *in* TOYLAND

·························

Pet supply stores cater to cat lovers who want to pamper their pets. There are tons of kitty toys available in every price range. Feline toys fall into four categories:

- Toys that dish out rewards, such as puzzle feeders

- Toys that encourage exploration, such as tunnels

- Toys that demand to be chased, such as crinkle balls or catnip creatures on wands

- Toys that test intelligence, such as remote-control mice or the peek-a-prize puzzle (a nifty box with several holes through which a cat can paw out treats and toys)

You can always make your own **cat toys out of** common household items, too:

- Crumpled wads of paper

- Shoelaces, heavy string, or yarn

- Large paper bags from the grocery or department store

- A tent of newspapers

- A cardboard box with a few holes cut in the sides

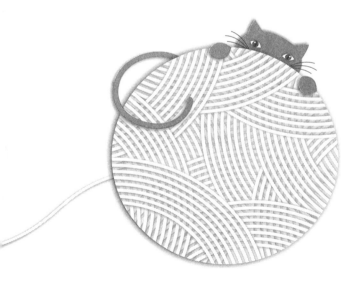

Need yet another reason to quit smoking? Do it out of love for your cat. Recent studies confirm that secondhand smoke bothers cats, too. In fact, one in five cats suffers from some type of allergy, including

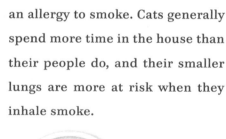

an allergy to smoke. Cats generally spend more time in the house than their people do, and their smaller lungs are more at risk when they inhale smoke.

FUNNY FELINES

....

Laughing at your cat's antics can be good for your health — no joke. And look at all the famous funny felines throughout cartoon history: Felix the Cat, Krazy Kat, Tom (and Jerry, of course), Sylvester, Garfield, Catbert (the evil human resources director in *Dilbert*), and many others.

The next time you're chuckling at something humorous (feline or otherwise), share the joke with your cat. He may not comprehend the punch line, but he'll enjoy hearing your happy voice.

There is something special about having your cat hop up onto the bed to find a comfy spot to snooze with you. If you need to shift positions during the night, do it slowly and gently. Your cat will appreciate your consideration.

TERRIFIC TIP

If you need to awaken your cat,
whisper his name first. Allow
his eyes to open before you touch
his body so that you don't startle
him and risk incurring an
unintended scratch.

Curb sleep-disturbing nighttime play by outfoxing your feline. She may sleep through the night if you try the following:

- Change her feeding time from early morning to right before bed. A full belly helps a cat to snooze longer through the night.

- Spend 20 minutes or so before bedtime playing with your cat so that she will be ready to go to sleep when you are.

- Gently awaken your slumbering cat periodically during the day and engage her in spirited play to tire her out.

Find the cause of your cat's mischief. Only then can you take the appropriate steps to improve her behavior. Never physically punish your cat. If she is anxious to begin with, physical punishment will only worsen the situation. Instead of paying attention to bad behavior, give "bonuses" for good behavior.

For example, dole out treats and praise when your cat comes on cue and sits pretty. Ignore your cat when she paws at you while you are trying to type on the keyboard. If you stop and push away her paw, she gets what she wanted: attention.

FUN *with* FEATHERS

....

Buy a handful of peacock feathers and attach them to the end of a flexible pole. Then flag your cat's attention. Feathers are usually too much of a temptation to resist. In no time, your cat will be running, jumping, and performing amazing body twists and turns to snag those moving feathers.

The next time you curl up in the recliner to read a chapter or two from your favorite novel, welcome your cat on your lap. Read out loud to her. She may not be able to decipher the author's plot or prose, but the sound of your voice is welcoming to her. She enjoys your attention, and you have to keep reading as long as she is snoozing there — a good excuse not to do chores or errands!

If you adopted a cat from an animal shelter, that's paws-itively great! But don't make that your last visit to a shelter. In appreciation for your new feline friend, find some time to help other less fortunate kitties:

- Become an adoption counselor and help pair people with cats to make a good union.

- Become an animal socializer and play with cats to get them used to human handling.

- Become a foster parent and provide a temporary loving home for sheltered kittens or cats to build up their socialization skills and confidence.

If you're taxed for time, open your wallet and pamper shelter cats in these ways:

- Donate new collars, leashes, and bowls for food and water.

- Provide comfy blankets or beds.

- Take the money you would have spent going to the movies (don't forget the price of popcorn) and spend it at a pet supply store on toys and food for shelter cats. This act is rated PG — Pure Goodness!

Despite a common belief, cats cannot see in total darkness. Even though a cat's night vision is about six times stronger than a person's, be sure to have timers on a few lights, or use night lights with sensors that turn on as the room darkens, so that your senior cat can navigate easily when home alone in the evenings.

TERRIFIC TIP

Instead of constantly trying to shoo your cat off of your furniture, reach a compromise. Protect your furniture with a washable throw blanket or cotton sheet that you can remove once you return home.

No cat is perfect. For that matter, no person is either. Don't strive for perfection in your feline pal. Instead, practice accepting a cat's nature. Part of the fun of sharing life with a cat is that you can't script what will happen. Embrace those fun moments and even those moments of mischief — as long as your cat is not creating a *cat-astrophe*.

Catering to
Your Kitten

HAPPY CAT •
HAPPY YOU

Chapter
Two

KITTENS PUT THE "F" INTO FRISKY, FUN-LOVING, AND FRUSTRATING. THERE'S A REASON I DUB the first 12 months of a kitten's life the Wonder Year: You wonder where your kitten gets all that energy; you wonder how she managed to scale your drapes like a master mountain climber; you wonder when you will ever get a full night's sleep again. Kittens are anything but boring. They are full of wonder — and quite wonderful. Let's look at some ways to make your first year together the start of a lifelong friendship.

THE BASIC SUPPLIES

....

Make sure your kitten is off on the right paw by stocking up on feline necessities. The checklist includes food and water bowls, a litter box with unscented litter and scoop, a cushy bed, a collar, an identification tag, a sturdy scratching post, and toys and treats suitable for kittens.

Take steps to insure that your cat is a law-abiding feline citizen. Check with your health department about licensing rules that apply in your community. There may be regulations regarding identification tags and housing limits or restrictions.

HANDLE *with* CARE

....

The more safe and secure your kitten feels when you hold her, the more likely she is to enjoy being picked up and cuddled.

Cradle your kitten when you carry her to prevent the squirming youngster from falling. Use both hands to pick her up. Place one hand under her chest just behind her forelegs. Cradle her hind legs in one arm and let her forelegs rest on your other arm for comfort and safety. Show youngsters how to properly hold your kitten.

QUALITY TIME

....

Cats of all ages love to be loved by their favorite people. And it's okay to admit that you desire some TLC — Tabby Lap Cat. Encourage your kitten to be more affectionate by spending time playing with him — time that is more meaningful than you might think it would be.

After a vigorous play session, fast-growing kittens need to nap. Use that opportunity to place him on your lap. Gently stroke his head, ears, and back until he falls asleep. Stay put for a half hour or so and read a book or turn the television on low. These kitten-bonding moments go a long way in creating a cat who craves cuddling.

Consult with your veterinarian to select a high-quality food for your kitten. Remember that as your kitten grows, his dietary needs will change. By his first birthday, he will need to switch to an adult diet that meets his activity level and health condition. Always remember to measure out his daily portions to keep him at a fit weight.

WHO ARE YOU &
WHAT IS THAT?!

As cuddly cute as kittens are, they must be taught how to socialize. As soon as you bring your young feline home, you can begin instilling good manners, self-confidence, and trust in your newest addition to the family.

Expose your impressionable kitten to young people, old people, tall people, short people, people with accents, and people wearing hats and other funny clothes that make them look different.

If possible, your kitten should meet other cats and yes, even friendly d-o-g-s! Just make sure that your kitten is up to date on all her vaccinations before doing a paw-and-purr greet with any critters outside your home.

In addition to being introduced to other animals, your kitten needs to become used to her surroundings so that she doesn't develop phobias.

- Let her get used to the sounds of the vacuum cleaner, dishwasher, and hair dryer.

- Introduce her to her own reflection in mirrors.

- Hoist her onto the slick top of the clothes dryer (the surface simulates a veterinary clinic's exam table).

- Expose her to different surfaces, from slippery tile or wood flooring to plush carpet, from grass to a gravel driveway (a good opportunity to practice leash training, too!).

Animal behavior experts report that it isn't only puppies who benefit from organized classes taught by pet trainers.

In addition to learning to be handled and groomed, kittens gain confidence by exploring new places and having new experiences in a safe and supportive environment.

One common activity in kitten kindergarten is called "pass the kitty," during which each kitten is passed from one person to the next. These classes also teach kittens how to play nicely with other kittens. Check with your local animal shelter and veterinary clinic for a kitten kindergarten class in your area.

Kittens — and cats young at heart — are most active at dawn and dusk. That's because they are crepuscular, wired genetically to do their best hunting and play stalking during those times of day. Schedule play sessions with your cat during these times and let the fun fly!

SHOWING OFF

....

Is your purebred kitten too cute for words? Show her off to the world — the world of cat shows, that is. The Cat Fanciers' Association (*www.cfa.org*), the world's largest breed registry, sponsors shows of various types and levels of age and experience for the 41 breeds it recognizes. One of the judging classes caters to kittens (spayed/neutered or not) too young for championship class eligibility.

Consult the breeder from whom you obtained your kitten for details on shows. Good luck! May your kitten fetch a prize-winning ribbon!

TERRIFIC TIP

Make your hand a friend to your kitten right from the start. Never hit your kitten or he will learn to mistrust hands and may become fearful or aggressive.

HANDS OFF!

....

Resist playing "hand wrestling" with your kitten. It may be cute, but kittens can become overstimulated during play and start biting your hands, so use wand toys instead of your fingers as playthings. You don't want biting to become a habit because a full-grown cat can seriously injure you if he doesn't know when to stop.

If your kitten insists on using your hands for hunting practice, spray a little Bitter Apple on your hand or dab on some pickle juice. Reward good, quiet behavior with calm petting or a treat. Your kitten will soon learn that he reaps better dividends for good behavior.

All the toys in the world won't mean much to your kitten unless *you* play, too. A few minutes a day with you and a simple piece of string shows your feline friend that it is worth waking up from a catnap for playtime.

LET *the* GOOD TIMES ROLL

·················

You and your kitten can have a lot of fun with a remote-controlled mouse. Be sure to operate the remote so that the toy mouse moves in short bursts, changes directions, and stops suddenly, just like a real mouse. This sparks the predator instinct in your kitten, who will happily give chase.

Teach your kitty to come on cue by playing a version of hide-and-seek. Start by having your kitten next to you in a room. Throw a small treat across the room. As he darts after it, slip around the corner out of sight and call his name in an upbeat, cheery tone. When he races to you, reward him with a treat and plenty of praise. Repeat four or five times during a play session.

FISHING *for* MICE

. . . .

Hone your young cat's hunting skills by attaching a toy mouse to the end of a flexible pole with sturdy string. Toss the mouse within sight of your cat. When she slinks to the ground and arches up her backside, reel in the mouse. Let the fun begin! Move the mouse up and down and side to side to give your cat a good workout while she sharpens her stalking and pouncing skills.

Dim the lights and cast a beam on the walls and floor with a penlight, small flashlight, or laser pointer. Select an area free of breakable items and tippy furniture and bounce the light around in varying tempos and heights. Watch him take off in hot purr-suit — some cats really go crazy for this game.

WALK THIS WAY

....

Teach your kitten some doglike tricks and skills. Yes, a new kitten (and even some old cats) can be trained to wear a harness and walk on a leash. Buy a harness designed for cats. Look for woven nylon and quick-release (not breakaway) snaps and adjustable straps around the chest, belly, and neck that securely hug your cat and make it impossible for her to slip out and escape.

The secret is to make the harness and leash seem like no big deal and to take the process slowly and in small steps.

1. Let her investigate the new equipment by sniffing and perhaps pawing at it.

2. Gently put the harness on and shower her with praise and treats while you leave it on for 15 to 20 seconds and then remove it. Do this a few times and then leave the lesson for the next day.

3. Gradually build up the time and your kitten's positive association with the harness while still inside your house. After a while, attach the leash and let her drag it around.

4. Start following her while you hold the leash and begin to gently direct her movements from room to room.

5. Once you're both in stride, you can walk out to the mailbox together to fetch the mail. Just don't expect any cat to trot along at your heels — you'll have to let her set the pace and probably the route!

6. Pick a time of day when your neighborhood is quiet so that there will be fewer distractions for your exploring feline.

7. Practice patience. The first outings may last only a minute or two. Give your cat time to process the experience so that she feels safe and confident the next time out.

8. Cats are clock-watchers. Strive to take your outdoor walks around the same time of day, letting them become part of your cat's daily routine.

TERRIFIC TIP

Redirect play stalking and ankle
biting by rolling Ping-Pong balls
and paper wads down the hall.
Kittens can't resist the chance to
chase these inanimate forms of prey
throughout the house.

BATTING PRACTICE

. . . .

Some kittens were born big-league batters. Train your kitten to bat a Ping-Pong ball or paper wad back to you. You may need to swat these items to demonstrate this form of play game. When she paws the ball or paper wad in your direction, praise and treat to reinforce this desired action. Do this a few times a day and your kitten will soon associate paper wads and Ping-Pong balls with fun times to interact with you.

Throughout her first year, your kitten practices her instinctive predatory behaviors such as stalking, pouncing, and clawing. Recognize that your young kitten enters different mental states as she grows. During the first 12 weeks of life, kittens download a lot of information on appropriate play from their littermates. They learn about bite inhibition and other proper feline manners.

By four or five months, your young feline focuses more on playing chase, be it a toy mouse or a paper wad. When kittens reach puberty at around six months, their play style evolves into marking (scratching objects to leave their scent) and testing their dominance (which explains why your kitten is pouncing on your ankles).

SHAKE, RATTLE, *and* ROLL

....

Put a teaspoon of rice (uncooked, of course!) in an empty plastic film canister or medicine bottle and seal the cap with tape to prevent it from being pulled off. Roll it to your kitten when he is in a playful mood. The sound will probably prove irresistible, and he will quickly begin batting around this rattly toy.

TERRIFIC TIP

Before your kitten even crosses your threshold, set up several sturdy scratching posts in different rooms. This way, you can start off on the right claw by directing him to scratch on the posts instead of the sofa or the drapes.

Kitten-proof your home room by room. That means hiding or covering electrical cords, putting secure lids on trash cans, and installing childproof latches on floor-level cabinets.

Tidy up your desk and keep easy-to-swallow (and easy-to-choke-on) items such as paper clips, rubber bands, and buttons stored inside drawers or containers with lids.

Use boards to block the spaces around refrigerators and big appliances so your curious kitten cannot wiggle in and become trapped.

Size up your litter box to fit the size of your cat. Kittens need small boxes with low sides so that they can easily climb in and out. Giant litter boxes with sides four inches or higher, or ones featuring hoods, can be too uninviting — even a bit intimidating — for a youngster.

LITTER BOX LESSONS

. . . .

Although kittens may seem to be born knowing how to use a litter box, the truth is that they learn from their mothers. Play it safe by escorting your newly adopted feline to the litter box for the first few days. Place her inside the box and gently move her front paws through the litter to let her feel the texture. Let her explore this feline bathroom and jump out on her own. Keep her confined to one room with the box until she is using it reliably.

Tissues can be tempting to some young felines who take great delight in swiping them from the box and shredding them into confetti. It's a real boredom buster but makes for a big cleanup job. Nip this habit by turning tissue boxes upside down when not in use and trying to remember to close the bathroom door.

Of course, if you don't mind the mess, it's an awful lot of fun for your kitten!

Does your kitten love to leap, especially when you are trying to catch up on the latest news in your local paper? Read your favorite sections without interruption by taking a few sheets from the sections you aren't reading and propping them up like a paper tent on the floor next to you. Tap the sides to attract your kitten's attention or hide a favorite small toy under the pages. He will enjoy leaping and diving while you scan the headlines in peace.

A CAT CONNECTION

....

Cathy Conheim, a lifelong dog devotee, adopted an abandoned kitten named Henry who needed surgery to remove his damaged front left leg. She began writing of Henry's exploits to friends in e-mails. The response was so overwhelming that she wrote a book called *What's the Matter with Henry?* Today, this three-legged feline has thousands of "paw pals" all across the globe. Check out his Web site at *www.henrysworld.org*.

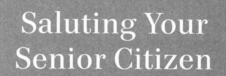

Saluting Your
Senior Citizen

Chapter
Three

HAPPY CAT
HAPPY YOU

WHERE DID ALL THE YEARS GO? IT'S EASY TO BE CAUGHT CATNAPPING REGARDING YOUR cat's senior citizen status. Unlike dogs, cats don't sport gray muzzles or other obvious clues of advancing age. They may still retain a kittenlike playfulness or appear to be lapping from the Feline Fountain of Youth, but you've probably noticed some signs of slowing down. Discover how you can make their golden years a time to treasure.

Treat your aging cat like a CEO: Cat Extra-Ordinaire. Your cat has been loyal to you since kittenhood. Now is the time to increase her daily dose of pampering. One easy way is to warm a small blanket in the clothes dryer for 5 to 10 minutes and then drape it on your cat during chilly nights to help her to fall asleep. You can also put a warm blanket on your arthritic cat during the day to help improve blood flow and ease muscle aches.

CREATURE COMFORTS

....

Place water bowls in different locations around the house. Older cats tend to drink less, but with water readily available your cat is less likely to become dehydrated.

Drinking a lot more than usual, however, can be a sign of kidney disease or diabetes, so monitor the water level to determine how much your cat is drinking. Report any dramatic changes in water consumption to your veterinarian.

If your cat isn't in a social mood, let her have her own space. Older cats tend to sleep more than frisky youngsters do and may be somewhat less tolerant of unwanted attention. If you have a younger cat who wants to play, stop a feline feud by ensuring that your senior cat has a safe and private place to snooze.

Bring on the beef, heap on the fish, and pile on the chicken. Most senior cats require extra protein in order to maintain lean body mass and a strong immune system.

The exception: older cats with kidney dysfunction need low-protein prescription diets. Work with your veterinarian to choose the right diet.

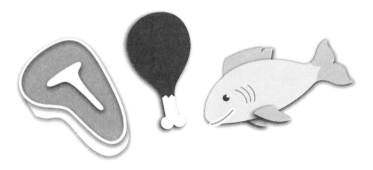

TERRIFIC TIP

Many senior cats still possess a kitten's desire to play, so continue daily exercise. Just go more slowly with the catnip mouse or pole-chase toy and shorten playtime. Be sure to let her catch the toy so that she can feel that her hunting skills are still working.

Take a preventive approach to ensure that your cat enjoys a long, healthy life. After your cat's seventh birthday, schedule a comprehensive checkup that includes blood and urine samples. The results will provide a baseline of your cat's condition and help your vet to customize her care as she ages.

Book wellness exams every six months to monitor her health. When age-related conditions such as diabetes or arthritis are detected early on, treatment can be maximized.

Look for early signs of senility in your aging cat. Work with your veterinarian on suitable treatments. DISH is a handy acronym to help scope out your cat's cognitive abilities:

Disorientation. Signs include a cat who stares at walls or seems to get "stuck" in corners.

Interaction. Affected cats don't greet people when they come home or seek out a lap as they did before.

Sleep. Cats who once slept through the night may roam the house restlessly and howl.

House soiling. Some senile cats forget to use the litter box.

One clue that your aging cat is not feeling well is that his once-shiny coat looks dull and may even have mats. Cats are fastidious groomers, but arthritis, injuries, and illnesses may affect their abilities to keep their coats healthy. Aid your cat by brushing his coat regularly. Brushes lift and remove loose hair that can cause hairballs. The act of brushing also improves circulation and triggers oil secretion, which keeps the coat healthy.

If you have an indoor-outdoor enclosure for your cat that features a stiff plastic door flap, replace it with a piece of thick cloth. The reason? Older cats may not have the muscle needed to push open the flap to go in and out safely.

Once a month, smell your cat's breath. "Doggy breath" could be a sign of problems with the gums or teeth or could indicate another health condition. Inspect her teeth for signs of tartar buildup and chipped or missing teeth. Consult your vet about dental care for your aging cat.

THE CAT'S MEOW

....

February is National Pet Dental Month. Some veterinarians offer a discount on dental exams and services. So, *do* be down in the mouth, for your cat's sake!

For an arthritic cat, capsules containing glucosamine and chondroitin (these supplements work best as a team) to improve mobility and joint lubrication can be incorporated into his diet. You can sprinkle the contents from the capsule into your cat's canned food or, as a treat, mix with a bit of canned tuna. Ask your vet for dosage information.

Keep your cat's sleeping area warm and cozy. Position a bed near a source of warmth — near a sunny window or by the fireplace or next to a heat vent. Grab your comforter and a good book and spend some time with your snoozing friend while you pamper yourself with some quiet time as well.

MEOW MEOW meow MEOW MEOW MEOW MEOW MEOW ME OW meow meow meow

LOOK WHO'S TALKING

....

Older cats can become quite chatty — out of confusion. Be patient with them and talk back to them to provide a sense of comfort.

Senior cats deserve to have litter boxes on each level of your home, especially if they have arthritis, which can make moving up and down stairs difficult. Be sure these feline bathrooms are located in easy-to-access places and are not near noisy appliances.

Also be aware that stiffer joints make climbing in and out of a deep box more challenging. Your cat might appreciate boxes with lower sides.

CELEBRATING SENIORS

. . . .

May is Older Americans Month, and the Humane Society of the United States uses this event to highlight the health benefits of pets for the elderly.

November is Adopt a Senior Pet Month, sponsored by Petfinder.com.

Identify friends and relatives who have cats seven years or older and send them a greeting card, or make a donation in your senior cat's name to a favorite feline charity.

The sense of smell in cats can fade with age, which in turn can diminish interest in eating. To spark your senior cat's appetite, make his meal more tempting by warming it in the microwave for a few seconds before serving. This brings out the food's full aroma and makes it more alluring to your cat.

TERRIFIC TIP

If your older cat isn't keeping up with his grooming, occasionally work a small amount of baking soda into his coat with your fingers. It's a natural odor absorber that isn't harmful to cats.

HOW OLD IS THAT *in* CAT YEARS?

....

Nix the notion that "one cat year equals seven human years"; it's fiction, not fact. In reality, a 1-year-old cat is roughly equivalent to a 15-year-old person. By age 7, cats reach senior status and by age 12 are considered geriatric. Here's a chart that shows your senior cat's age in approximate people years:

Cat's Age	People Years	Cat's Age	People Years
7	44	14	72
8	48	15	76
9	52	16	80
10	56	17	84
11	60	18	88
12	64	19	92
13	68	20	96

Install ramps or foot stools to help your arthritic or aging cat up the stairs or onto the bed. The best choices are wide enough to meet your cat's needs and feature nonslip surfaces for greater traction. Bedtime bonding is a special time for your lifelong feline buddy, so make sure that he can easily get up onto your bed and snuggle next to you as you both drift off into snoozeland.

RIP VAN WINKLES

. . . .

Only bats and opossums sleep more than cats, who average 18 to 20 hours of sleep each day. A 15-year-old cat has most likely spent 10 years of his life sleeping!

Take a cue from your cat and aim for 8 to 9 hours of sleep each night. During sleep, your body goes into repair mode, and when you wake up, you will feel refreshed and ready to take on the day's challenges.

Advanced age can lead to deafness in your cat. Some deaf cats still have their wits about them but become quite vocal because they cannot hear their own voices. It's just not possible to control the volume of their *meow*s.

Indicate on your cat's identification tag that she is deaf, and attach a bell to her collar to make it easier to find her in the house; after all, she is no longer able to come when you call.

WAKE-UP CALL

. . . .

Never approach a deaf cat without warning —
you don't want to startle her and have her swipe
at you out of fear. Tap the floor near her as you
approach so that she can feel the vibrations. Make
eye contact before petting her.

Make a point of monitoring your older cat's eating habits. A lack of interest in food or weight loss in spite of normal eating can indicate medical problems. Spend a moment gently stroking your cat while she eats (unless she objects to being petted while dining).

TERRIFIC TIP

Buy your old friend a cushy beanbag or a cozy bed with plenty of extra padding. You can also find cat beds made of memory foam. A thick sheepskin is another great way to keep kitty warm and to cushion stiff joints.

The beauty of older cats is that they tend to prefer cuddling to the roughhousing that kittens enjoy. If you are thinking about adding a cat to your feline household, please consider selecting an older cat from a shelter or breed rescue group. These cats will usually be up-to-date on all their vaccinations, and their personalities will already be known.

Multi-Cat Merriment

How Not to Be the

Crazy Cat Lady

HAPPY CAT ·

HAPPY YOU

Chapter Four

CATS ARE A LOT LIKE THOSE FAMOUS POTATO CHIPS: YOU CAN'T BE SATISFIED WITH JUST one. Most cats won't admit it, but they like being in the company of their peers. If you're away a lot or sense that your cat is tired of being a solo act, pair her up with a furry playmate. Many cats become quite comfortable with a feline friend or two and will form close relationships, while others can coexist quite well without doing more than offering one another a brief hello.

But just like a house of cards, adding one cat too many can upset household harmony. Paw through these pages to find out how to handle a multi-cat home, bring home a new addition to the family, and maintain peace among your pets.

TWO'S COMPANY

. . . .

Here's some news sure to make you purr. Studies confirm that cats lead healthier, more contented lives if there is another friendly cat in the house.

When seeking to adopt, why not bring home a pair of kittens from the same litter or a pair of adult cats who now find themselves in a shelter? These cats have already formed a friendship bond, and you will be saving two lives instead of one.

When two cats give each other full-body rubs, the action translates into: "There's strength in numbers; let's create a group odor for identification." My cats Callie and Murphy frequently do the mutual torso rub maneuver when they meet each other in the hallway.

KITTY HOUSE CALLS

. . . .

Rather than haul several cats to the veterinary clinic, you could seek the services of a veterinarian who makes house calls. Find a visiting vet in your area by contacting the American Association of Housecall & Mobile Veterinarians (*www.housecall vets.org*).

House calls are ideal solutions for multi-cat households, for people who don't drive, for those with little free time, and for senior citizens in assisted-living situations. The benefit for your cats is the opportunity to be examined on their home turf, a far less stressful environment than a clinic.

Know your financial and emotional limit for pets. Think quality, not quantity, when it comes to the number of animals who share your home. Remember that there is no such thing as a "free" feline. When deciding whether to add another cat to your home, take out your calculator in addition to your heart. On average, each cat costs at least $600 a year in routine care and feeding.

SHARE YOUR LOVE

....

If you love felines of all shapes and sizes, consider contacting your local animal shelter about becoming a foster parent. This way, you can have one or two of your own cats and rotate in one or two shelter cats who can benefit from being socialized in a home setting. Being fostered often bolsters their prospects of landing permanent homes.

If your resident cats have formed a tight friendship bond and don't tolerate temporary feline visitors, look for an extra "cat fix" by volunteering at your local animal shelter. You can provide a few hours a week of one-on-one time to cats and kittens up for adoption in the center's cat social room.

Embrace sharing your life with cats who are not "Siamese twins" in looks or attitudes. Celebrate that one of your cats may be a lap lover while the other thrives on performing gymnastic stunts to your applause.

BRINGING HOME *a* NEW CAT

....

Here are some ways to insure a proper introduction without a lot of hissing or flying fur:

1. Before you pick up the new member of the family, set up temporary housing for him in a small room, ideally a bathroom, with food, water, a litter box, and a place to sleep.

2. When you come home, take the new pet directly to the prepared bathroom. The goal here is not to let the resident cat(s) know that it was *you* who brought in this interloper.

3. At first, just allow the cats to sniff each other under the doorframe. Don't react to hissing or growling.

4. Spend one-on-one time with each pet, making sure that they each feel special.

5. After a day or two, put your first cat into the enclosed bathroom for a couple of hours while letting the new pet explore each room of the house under your supervision. This helps to neutralize any turf battles.

6. Take a slightly damp towel and rub it down your new pet's body. Then rub this towel on your first cat's body to mingle their scents.

7. After a few days, let your first cat roam free in a larger room while you bring in the new pet in a carrier or on a leash, and allow the first cat to approach and sniff.

8. Use positive reinforcement by offering bits of food each time you increase the exposure of the animals to each other. Always give a treat to your first cat before the newcomer receives one.

9. Allow the pets to be together in the same room only when you can supervise until you are sure that they get along. This can take a few days or a few weeks or even months, depending on the dynamics.

Your first choice for a second cat should be a kitten, preferably of the opposite sex. But great friendships can form between two adult cats, two cats of the same sex, and even cats and members of other species, such as dogs, guinea pigs, birds, and rabbits. If your cat has strong predator instincts, don't pair her up with rodents, birds, or rabbits.

Try to pair complementary personalities. If your cat is bold and outgoing, try matching her with a cat who is easygoing and willing to be a follower, not a leader.

If your cat has a favorite snoozing spot or is partial to a particular scratching post, provide the new cat with an alternative so that your original cat won't feel threatened by having to share. Making sure the first cat continues to feel comfortable will go a long way in easing the transition.

CAT PALS

....

Recognize that cats, just like people, have likes and dislikes when it comes to other cats. Cat A may be best pals with Cat B but do everything she can to avoid being around Cat C. Some feline friendships form in nanoseconds and others can take weeks, even months. As long as the two aren't harming each other, let them work out who is boss, once you have introduced them properly.

Study your cats' interactions, and do not try to force introductions or friendships. Some cats may never become best buds, but they may learn to accept one another.

LITTER BOX LORE

....

You don't need to be a math whiz to bring out the best bathroom behavior in your multi-cat household. The ideal formula is one litter box per cat, plus one. So if you have three cats, you need to have at least four litter boxes in your home.

Place the boxes strategically in different locations in the house. Scooping each box daily will reduce the risk of litter box boycotts due to behavior issues.

TERRIFIC TIP

Provide fresh water daily in a few
bowls placed around the house.
Clean the bowls regularly to prevent
bacteria from building up.

Keep a selection of various cat toys and rotate a handful of them each week to your brood. Be aware that not all toys are feline safe. Steer clear of these toys and materials:

- Toys with tiny parts or glued-on pieces, such as plastic eyes, that pose a choking hazard.

- Soft foam balls that can be easily shredded into small pieces. (Ditto for those lightweight "packing peanuts.")

- Plastic bags, especially the handled type from the supermarket. Many cats like to lick these, but they could choke or even become trapped inside and suffocate.

- Empty cigarette wrappers. The cellophane or foil wrapper can cause choking.

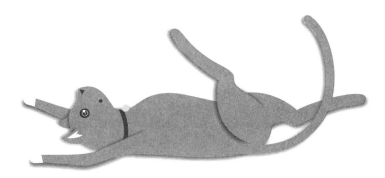

Catnip is caviar for cats. **A few times a week, make it "catty hour" for your feline pack by treating them to fresh organic catnip.**

Serve catnip on a paper plate or a throw rug, or sprinkle it on a scratching post. Make sure they have plenty of elbow room because in no time they will be salivating, rolling, rubbing, and leaping. Stand back and enjoy this display of feline bliss.

Many cats react to catnip because of its active ingredient, called nepetalactone. It closely resembles a chemical found in the urine of female cats, which may explain why male cats seem more animated by catnip than do female cats.

FRESH FUN

....

Grow a crop of catnip in your outdoor garden or in a room in the house that's off-limits to your cats. When offered to cats, the fresher, the better. Chop or crush the leaves and stems slightly to release the full aroma before serving about a teaspoonful to each of your cats.

Create homemade toys by filling a knotted piece of fabric or an old cotton sock with dried catnip. When the catnip loses its zip, just refill the toy with a fresh helping.

One way to maintain **peace in a multi-cat household** is to ensure that each cat has plenty of space, so take a tiered approach to your home. Tall cat trees, cat gyms, and cat condos with several levels enable cats to share the same piece of furniture without having to be elbow-to-elbow.

Sit on the floor and encourage your cats to gather around you by waving a wand toy or feather toy on the floor. Once you have their attention, let each one demonstrate his pouncing and nabbing skills. These group games sneak in some socialization for all felines. By doing this on a regular basis, your crew will gather on cue and learn to wait their turns for play.

BREED PERSONALITY TRAITS

If you like a particular breed, consider adopting a second one of similar heritage. Learn more about your favorite breed from the Cat Fanciers' Association (*www.cfa.org*), which recognizes more than 40 breeds. To demonstrate the personality range among felines, here is a sampling of four breeds who possess very different "cat-titudes":

Bengals are never boring. These active, agile, and alert cats are known for their love of drinking water from a dripping faucet, taking showers with their owners, and perching confidently on top of doors. Be aware that Bengals chirp, chortle, and sometimes howl.

The nearly hairless *Sphynx*, a definite head-turner in the feline world, has often been described as a combination of a cat, dog, and monkey. These people-adoring cats are playful and curious. They like to investigate cabinets, closets, and computer keyboards.

The tail-less *Manx* likes to follow favorite people like a puppy dog. They are good candidates to train to walk on leashes and to come on cue. They embrace feline buddies, with and without tails.

The *Cornish Rex* is regarded as the Golden Retriever of the feline scene. This breed loves to play fetch and comes racing when you call.

TERRIFIC TIP

Opt for more than one locale for feeding areas. With food bowls in different rooms, a shy cat can eat in peace while a bully cat finds that he can't be in two places at one time.

Keep your feline friends fit by teaching them the sport of agility. The Cat Fanciers' Association has sanctioned agility as a sport for cats. If your cats are not keen on traveling to participate in these organized events, you can create an indoor obstacle course for them by using household furnishings such as sturdy boxes, ramps, dining room chairs, and hollow tubes.

Counter feelings of stress in your cat crew with over-the-counter products such as Feliway, a product that mimics feline pheromones. It comes in a plug-in diffuser and a spray bottle. You can spray Feliway on cat bedding and cat trees to calm feline stress when there is disruption in the household routine.

CLEANLINESS
IS *a* GROUP EFFORT

. . . .

In a multi-cat household where harmony is king, chances are good that all of your cats will sport clean ears and coats. Close cat pals enjoy treating each other to grooming sessions, zeroing in on hard-to-reach places.

Recognize that cats are pioneers in the time-sharing concept. Cat A may commandeer the cat tree in the morning while Cat B lays claim to this piece of feline real estate in the afternoon. They seem to magically work out ways to live together and share possessions — including you!

Purr-fecting
Feline Décor

Chapter
Five

HAPPY CAT
HAPPY YOU

. . . .

THESE DAYS, WITH FAST-MOVING CARS AND HUNGRY COYOTES AND OTHER CRITTERS, IT'S "in" to be an indoor cat — and a lot safer. You can make your home a castle for an indoor cat without a lot of renovation or expense. And why not? Your cat logs more time inside your house than you do.

Pamper your feline a bit by adding a dash of *fang shui* to your overall décor. The idea is to make your cat so pleased and contented that the thought of shredding your sofa out of sheer boredom won't enter her feline mind.

. . . .

Extend the life of your cat by keeping her indoors. Indoor cats live an average of 12 to 18 years, while outdoor cats live an average of 5 to 6 years. They are at risk for being hit by vehicles, killed by coyotes and other cat-hunting predators, and subjected to Mother Nature's weather extremes.

TERRIFIC TIP

Learn how to make your cat's indoor life fun, and safe, by visiting the Indoor Cat Initiative Web site sponsored by the Ohio State University's College of Veterinary Medicine at www.indoorcat.org.

If a cat had the option of living in a long, narrow space shaped like a bowling lane or a vertical place shaped like a telephone booth, the booth would win every time. Cats enjoy being able to safely survey the scene from on high. You can curb a lot of cat mis-behaviors, such as scratching furniture or climbing on counters, by placing cat trees and cat-welcoming shelves in a few key places in your home.

SPECIAL SPOTS

. . . .

Cats love to curl up in out-of-the-way spots; you never know where you might find them taking a catnap. Some feline favorites include the bathroom sink (or even the tub — sans suds, of course), closet shelves, laundry baskets, and cozy corners behind big chairs or sofas. Any empty cardboard box will usually attract the cat of the house as well.

Offer your cat a feline hideaway by opening the bottom drawer of a dresser, preferably one you don't use regularly. Place an old towel on top of the items inside to keep them clean and hair-free. Don't close the drawer without checking for a purring occupant!

CAT *and* COMPUTER MOUSE

....

If your cat loves to supervise as you work at your computer (and by supervise, I mean "sit right in front of the monitor or walk back and forth on the keyboard"), try providing her with her own bed on a corner of your desk or other off-the-floor spot nearby where she can curl up but still keep an eye on you. Take a moment to play or cuddle when she first comes looking for you, but then plop her in her own place.

WINDOW ON THE WORLD

....

Purchase or construct a kitty perch to attach to a windowsill. Size up your cat so that the perch is wide and sturdy enough to accommodate even the biggest of tabbies. Position it on a window overlooking a bird feeder or with a view of the road so that she can keep tabs of the neighborhood comings and goings.

According to Japanese mythology, the feline sym-
bolizes protection against evil spirits. Bring good
fortune into your home by placing a ceramic feng shui
cat in a place safe from paw's reach. These figurines
come in different colors to beckon different energies.
For example, a white cat attracts good health while a
pink cat brings love and happiness.

BRINGING *the* OUTSIDE IN

. . . .

You can safely treat your indoor cat to the sights, sounds, and smells of the great outdoors. One simple solution is to install a window enclosure that juts off the building. These are typically the size of an air conditioner and can be customized to suit any housing situation from a suburban kitchen window to an apartment balcony. Premade models are available or you can build one yourself out of plywood, chicken wire, and PVC pipe.

If you have a yard, you can build an enclosed run where your cat can spend time on pleasant days (an existing dog run would work fine; just make sure that there are no cat-sized gaps for him to wiggle through). Provide a sturdy chair to perch on and a big branch or log for climbing and clawing.

FOILING *the* COUNTER-SURFING CAT

....

It's impossible to keep a determined cat off of your kitchen counters just by watching him. Most cats learn very quickly that you will shoo them off, so they just wait until you aren't around.

You can make kitchen counters less desirable by placing double-sided sticky tape on them — cats hate having sticky paws. Or fill a large cookie sheet with water and place it on the counter as a booby trap. Your leaping cat will land with an unceremonious splash and then quickly depart to dry off.

Or you can go high tech and invest in a motion detector that emits a burst of pressurized air when triggered — guaranteed to startle any cat and make that countertop unappealing.

CLAWS UP!

Cats scratch your furniture not because they are being malicious but because they have an innate need to sharpen their claws. When they scratch, they leave their scent behind, which brings them back to the same spot again and again.

Thwart your cat by spraying a neutralizing solution to remove this odor. Then apply double-sided sticky tape, heavy plastic, or aluminum foil to the arms of the furniture or drape a big towel or blanket over the arms.

That's Part 1. Part 2 calls for you to redirect your feline friend to practice "cat scratch fever" on a scratching post instead.

All scratching posts are not created equal. Look for these must-have features:

Stability. The post should be able to handle your cat's weight without toppling over.

Stretch. Cats like to stretch to scratch — a good post is tall enough or long enough to permit full extension of the paws.

Surface. Try a variety of materials and textures to see what your cat prefers. Options include carpeting, sisal fiber, corrugated cardboard, or a sturdy log with the bark still attached.

Place the post in an area where your cat likes to hang out, so that it's within claw's reach when your cat has the itch to scratch. Having two or three scratching posts provides plenty of choices other than your furniture.

Once your cat has claimed a particular spot, the scent he leaves with every scratching session will keep bringing him back, but you can sprinkle some organic catnip on the post once a week to refresh his interest.

CAT BURGLARS

. . . .

Many cats are attracted to small, shiny objects that are easily batted around or carried in the teeth. To prevent a choking accident, not to mention the risk of losing your valuables, stash earrings, rings, cuff links, and necklaces in fastened jewelry boxes out of paws' reach.

Keep rubber bands, buttons, thumbtacks, and other small items in drawers or containers. Store loose change in narrow-necked bottles. Be very careful not to leave needles and thread lying around after a sewing project.

CURSES — FOILED AGAIN!

For cats who like to eliminate in houseplant dirt, take away the opportunity by placing aluminum foil over the exposed dirt in your potted plants. Try using gold or red decorative foil to add a splash of color to your greenery.

It may seem as though cats do nothing but sleep (and they do sleep an awful lot), but it's important to realize that napping can take place out of sheer boredom. Provide feline amenities such as a cat playhouse or a kitty condo that offer places to climb and hide and come with toys such as a feather teaser and dangling bell ball. Sure, your cat might nap there too, but at least he'll have other options.

TERRIFIC TIP

Stash some cedar chips in the washable cover of your cat's bedding. Fleas detest the cedar smell.

Occupy your cat's solo time by filling special treat balls and hiding them around the house. While you're away, your cat can hone her predatory drive. She will focus on the hunt and not have the time or desire to destroy things out of boredom or anxiety.

WHAT CATS WATCH

....

Provide your cat with must-see feline TV by installing a lifelike aquarium screen saver on your computer monitor or by playing cat-appropriate DVDs on your television set while you're away from home. Or set a timer to turn your television on during the day if there is a program that your cat pays attention to (perhaps something on the Discovery Channel or Animal Planet).

If you really want to keep your cat's attention, you could set up a live aquarium with a few colorful fish. Just be sure that the lid is securely fastened to prevent snacking and spilling!

LET'S TALK LITTER

Since litter box issues are by far the most common reason that cats are taken to shelters, it's important that you figure out what works best for your cat(s) so that you can all live harmoniously without litter box hassles and problems.

Litter boxes are enjoying a revolution in design and features. Nowadays they come in all sizes and shapes, with hoods and domes to provide privacy and enclosures that make them fit for the living room. Some even clean themselves!

Cats are like Felix of **The Odd Couple**; they like things neat. Here's the scoop on litter box success:

- Fill the box with litter to a depth of three inches.

- Don't use perfumed litters — we may think that they smell good, but most cats hate flowery scents. Similarly, don't use a plug-in air freshener in the vicinity (try an old-fashioned box of baking soda instead).

- Clean out deposits every day.

- Wash the litter box once a month with warm, soapy water and allow it to dry completely.

- Don't play hide-and-seek with the litter box. Cats are creatures of habit and don't like changes.

- Never place the litter box next to your cat's food or water bowls. Cats don't like to eat near their bathroom spot.

- Keep the box away from noisy appliances such as the washer and dryer that might discourage a timid cat.

PLAY IT AGAIN, SAM

. . . .

Keep the radio playing on low volume. Some cats
like jazz or classical music; others prefer talk radio.
Dial in to your cat's preference.

TERRIFIC TIP

If the best spot for the litter box is in a corner that traps odors, position a small oscillating fan (on low) near the litter box to ventilate the area. Make sure that it doesn't blow directly on the box, though; cats may not like their hair ruffled while they're using the box.

If you're truly cat-crazy, **think about installing a catwalk on brackets along a wall of your family room or bedroom. It should be 6 to 12 inches wide and hang about 2 feet below the ceiling. Provide access with a couple of perches from which to scale the heights. Most cats adore the opportunity to explore the upper strata.**

CAUTION: CURIOUS CATS

....

Be aware of and remove potential household dangers for a curious, leaping cat:

- A hot iron left on an ironing board

- A lightweight lamp on a corner table

- A dangling electric cord

- A vase of cut flowers

Love the look of greenery in your home? Unfortunately, lots of cats love houseplants, too, but they can get sick, and even die, from eating certain plants. Making the top poisonous-to-cats list are:

- Azalea
- Daffodil bulbs
- Dieffenbachia
- Geranium
- Holly
- Impatiens
- Ivy
- Mistletoe
- Morning glory
- Oleander
- Philodendron
- Poinsettia

For a complete list of no-no plants, click on the Humane Society of the United States' Web site at *www.hsus.org*.

Compromise by using silk plants (hey, no need to water) or plants deemed safe for cats looking to munch some greenery. Here is a sampling of cat-friendly plants to spruce up your home:

- Begonia
- Chamomile
- Fern
- Lavender
- Peppermint
- Spider plant
- Violet
- Zinnia

Make all greenery anything but tempting for your feline by hoisting plants on ceiling hooks where they'll be inaccessible to even the most gymnastic of cats.

TERRIFIC TIP

Place a cat bed in a tucked-away area of the living room. The bed is your cat's refuge, but it also keeps him within sight of family activities.

Satisfy your cat's curiosity by letting her sniff around your closet while you're deciding what to wear. Some cats love to explore a usually off-limits space, such as the attic or a basement. Just don't forget and lock her up in there.

SUNNY SIDE UP

. . . .

Nothing says relaxation like the sight of a sacked-out cat snoozing in a puddle of sunshine. Make a point of opening the blinds on sunny days so that your cat can indulge in this favorite pastime.

Place safety stickers on your front and back windows that indicate the number and types of pets in your home as a way to alert the police or firefighters in case of an emergency, such as a house fire. Your local animal shelter, police station, or firehouse may have a supply of these stickers, or you can obtain them from The Humane Society of the United States (*www.hsus.org*).

Locate a sturdy scratching post in your bedroom so that your cat spots it when she wakes up. My cat, Murphy, enjoys a morning ritual of a little TLC, a leisurely stretch, and a good scratch to limber up for the day. Naturally, I praise her to reinforce this habit.

Kitty Cuisine
for Finicky
Felines

HAPPY CAT •
HAPPY YOU

Chapter
Six

C ATER TO YOUR CAT AT CHOWTIME BY FEEDING HER THE RIGHT AMOUNT OF THE RIGHT FOOD. That may be easier said than done. After all, when a pair of soulful eyes is aimed your way, it's human nature to heap on the helpings — or to skip the kibble and serve table scraps.

Show true love by resisting the urge to overfeed your cat. We all like to indulge our pets, but we're slowly killing them with kindness. Each extra ounce of body fat reduces your cat's life span, mobility, and vitality. What you put in your cat's food bowl plays a big part in your cat's health — and longevity. *Bone* appétit!

Never underestimate the power of pure water. Cats lack thumbs, making it futile for them to attempt to twist open the cap on a water bottle. They need your help to stay hydrated so replenish their water bowl daily with filtered or bottled water. Become the cat's meow and jazz up the old water hole by providing your cat with a large-capacity pet fountain that aerates the water continuously.

As a card-carrying carnivore, your cat fares best when real meat tops the list of ingredients in his food bowl. Select premium brands of cat food that list a real protein such as turkey, chicken, or lamb as the first ingredient and avoid brands that list by-products, cornmeal, or other grains first.

Take the guesswork out of feline food shopping by reading labels carefully. Look at the percentages of protein, fat, and fiber. Choose food sanctioned by the American Association of Feed Control Officials (AAFCO). The AAFCO seal indicates that the product has passed rigorous feeding trials for balanced nutrition.

Look for these feline-fine nutrients:

- Vitamin E
- Protein
- Beta-carotene
- L-carnitines
- Gamma linolenic acid
- Glucosamines
- Omega-3 fatty acids
- Fiber

Such nutrients contribute to overall health as well as helping to repair cartilage, rejuvenate dry skin, build muscle tissue, boost the immune system, and aid digestion.

TUBBY TABBY?

....

If you're starting to nickname your cat Porky Puss, do the obesity test. Place both thumbs on your cat's backbone and rub your fingers along her rib cage. If you can't feel her ribs through the flab, she's probably overweight.

Love sushi? So do I, but nix the notion of taking home a "doggy bag" for your kitty. Raw fish runs the risk of harboring parasites and other nasty stuff that can upset a cat's stomach. A safer substitute: offer your cat an occasional treat of cooked tuna or salmon. Cooking raw fish destroys an enzyme that can deplete thiamine, an important B vitamin that all cats need.

Take the ho-hum out of your cat's commercial dry food by adding a splash of tuna juice or salt-free chicken broth to the bowl. After this saucy feast, your feline may spend extra time savoring these special extras during her post-meal grooming sessions because of the lingering delightful aromas from these feline "au jus" toppings.

ALL BUT *the* ROAR

....

Let your tabby feel like a lion by making him hunt for some of his daily calories. Try these techniques:

- Put a small dish of food up on a secure shelf so that he has to climb or jump for it.

- Insert a few spoonfuls of kibble into a food puzzle toy that he has to bat around. (This is an especially good idea when you're going to be out of the house for a while.)

- Rather than put your cat's kibble in a bowl at breakfast, place pieces on the stairs so that he has to climb up and down to eat his meal.

PLAYING *with* FOOD

....

Every once in a while, play a game by putting a dab of canned food or a special treat such as tuna in one spot and directing your cat's attention to it. Once he's gobbled that up, show him another dab in another spot. That way he has to travel for his treats and he'll be exercising while he eats.

TERRIFIC TIP

When teaching your cat a new trick, roll bits of canned food into little balls rather than relying on high-calorie commercial treats. Or cut lean, cooked meats into itty-bitty pieces (no bigger than the size of the nail on your little finger).

Treat cats of all ages to a pet vitamin that provides many important nutrients. Consult your veterinarian to select the right vitamin to meet your cat's age, health, and activity level. There are some chewable vitamin varieties, but not all cats are keen on those. For non-chewable vitamins, crush them into a powder so you don't have to feel like a sumo wrestler in trying to get the pill down your cat's throat.

NOT GOOD *for* CATS

. . . .

Even though cats don't have that canine reputation for inhaling anything that hits the kitchen floor, some people food should be on your cat's no-no list. Here are some foods that should be kept out of paw's reach:

Onions. Contain large amounts of sulfur, which can destroy red blood cells and cause severe anemic reactions in cats.

Garlic. Can damage a cat's red blood cells, especially in large quantities.

Grapes. Can cause choking.

Raw meat. Carries the threat of bacteria and parasites, possibly causing your cat to suffer diarrhea or vomiting.

Forgo the idea of a 24-hour food buffet when it comes to feeding your feline. Measure out daily portions and serve meals twice a day. This helps you to keep better tabs on how much food your cat is eating. You can tweak the portion amount to keep your cat at a healthy weight.

Check the expiration date on food labels and never serve any cat food past its prime. Unless you are feeding a whole kit and caboodle of cats, resist buying huge bags of dry food because it tends to go stale before your cat can eat all of the contents.

Make mealtime the ideal time to treat minor skin conditions such as feline flakes by adding a teaspoon of olive, corn, safflower, or sunflower oil to your cat's meal a few times a week. These oils help to replenish the body's natural oils and reduce dry, itchy skin.

SAFELY SHEDDING
the SURPLUS

....

Never put your fat cat on a crash diet. You run the risk of your cat losing more muscle mass than excess fat. Cats need food to metabolize their liver enzymes and can become quite ill after a couple of days of suddenly restricted food portions. Work with your veterinarian so that your cat can shed extra pounds slowly, steadily, and safely.

In general, gradually reduce the amount of chow you give your overweight cat by about 10 percent weekly. Cut back on the treats, too. These lip-smacking goodies should never account for more than 5 to 10 percent of your cat's total daily food intake.

It's fun to treat your cat to a homemade meal once in a while. Preparing a well-balanced, nutritionally complete, homemade diet can be tricky, however. Here are two pet nutrition Web sites operated by top veterinary nutritionists who deliver "meaty" advice on making healthy choices: *www.petdiets.com* and *www.balanceit.com*.

PREPARING KITTY CUISINE

. . . .

To really show your cat how much you love her, follow these tips for offering safe and healthy feline cuisine:

- Select fresh, and if possible, organically grown ingredients.

- Wash your hands in warm, soapy water before handling food.

- Clean all produce in cold water to wash away any pesticides, dirt, and bugs.

- Always cook meat, seafood, poultry, and eggs to reduce the risk of salmonella or parasitic threat.

- Trim fat from meats and drain excess grease from cooked meats.

- Store leftovers in airtight containers in the refrigerator for up to four days or in the freezer for up to three months.

FELINE FEASTS

. . . .

Want to win over your cat? **Treat** her to a special meal of homemade kitty cuisine. It's easier than you might imagine and is a great way to show your love and affection. Cats are true carnivores but diets enriched with veggies can offer added nutrition. Here are some recipes that have won over the hearts — and tummies — of my cat pals.

HEAVENLY KITTY HASH

....

To vary this recipe, **substitute barley for rice, flounder for ground turkey, or wheat-germ oil for corn oil. Makes 3 servings.**

> 1 cup water
>
> ⅓ cup uncooked brown rice
>
> 2 teaspoons corn oil
>
> pinch of salt
>
> ⅔ cup lean ground turkey
>
> 2 tablespoons chopped liver
>
> 1 tablespoon bonemeal

1. In a medium saucepan, bring the water to a boil. Stir in the rice, corn oil, and salt and reduce the heat to low. Allow the mixture to simmer for 20 minutes, covered.

2. Add the ground turkey, chopped liver, and bonemeal. Stir frequently and simmer for 20 more minutes.

COLOSSAL CAT CHOWDER

....

Your cats will meow for more of this mouthwatering dish. Makes 5 servings.

> ½ pound white fish, deboned and diced into small cubes
>
> 1 cup creamed corn
>
> 1 cup skim or low-fat milk
>
> ¼ cup red potato, finely chopped
>
> 1 tablespoon liver, finely chopped
>
> ¼ cup low-fat grated cheese

1. In a medium saucepan, combine all the ingredients except for the cheese. Cover and simmer over low heat for 20 minutes, stirring occasionally.

2. Remove from heat and sprinkle with cheese.

PURR-FECT TUNA PATTIES

....

For a simple variation on this feline-favorite recipe, substitute salmon, mackerel, or whitefish for the tuna. Makes 5 servings.

> 2 eggs
>
> One 6½-ounce can water-packed tuna, drained and flaked
>
> 1 cup bread crumbs
>
> 1 teaspoon brewer's yeast
>
> 1 teaspoon bonemeal
>
> pinch of salt
>
> 2 tablespoons margarine

1. In a medium-sized bowl, whip the eggs.

2. Add the tuna, bread crumbs, brewer's yeast, bonemeal, and salt. Blend with a wooden spoon until moistened.

3. In a skillet, melt the margarine over medium heat. Take small handfuls of the mixture and form 5 patties. Cook each side for 3 to 5 minutes or until golden brown.

4. When the patties have cooled, crumble them into small pieces.

SENSATIONAL KIDNEY STEW

....

This recipe contains an aromatic mix of kitty-pleasing foods. Makes 6 servings.

> 1½ cups water
>
> 1 tablespoon corn oil
>
> pinch of salt
>
> ½ pound beef kidney, diced
>
> ½ cup uncooked brown rice
>
> 1 medium carrot, finely grated
>
> 4 mushrooms, finely chopped
>
> 2 tablespoons tomato paste
>
> 1 teaspoon bonemeal

1. In a saucepan, combine the water, corn oil, and salt. Bring to a boil over medium heat.

2. Stir in the beef kidney, rice, carrot, mushrooms, and tomato paste and bring to a boil again.

3. Cover the saucepan, reduce the heat to low, and simmer for 20 minutes, stirring occasionally.

4. Remove from heat and add the bonemeal.

TABBY TUNA-SICLES

....

One 6½-ounce can water-packed tuna

Bottled water

1 teaspoon organic catnip, finely crushed

1. Drain the liquid from the tuna into a pouring cup.

2. Fill each space of a plastic ice cube tray halfway with the water.

3. Lightly sprinkle catnip into each of the cube holders.

4. Fill the rest of each cube holder with the tuna water.

5. Freeze until solid.

Plop one tuna-sicle into your cat's clean bowl and watch her enjoy this homemade fishy feast. Serve the drained tuna a couple of teaspoons at a time to liven up dry kibble.

TERRIFIC TIP

Keep your cat cool and occupied
during warm weather by putting
a few ice cubes into his water bowl.
Some felines get great glee out of
pawing at the ice cubes while
they drink.

Never buy low-fat cat food. **Fat helps to keep your cat's coat and skin healthy and gives him energy. The only issue with fat is that you shouldn't give too much.**

When it comes to burning calories, **size and shape count.** Small felines in general tend to burn calories faster than large cats do. Older, less active cats need fewer calories, while growing, active cats burn more calories.

You hate dirty dishes — well, so does your cat, even though she may have licked the platter clean! After each meal, wash your cat's food bowl in hot, soapy water and rinse thoroughly — or put it into the dishwasher — to prevent the growth of bacteria, such as *E. coli* and salmonella.

TERRIFIC TIP

Don't serve food or water in plastic
bowls. They are easier to tip over
and can impart an off flavor.
Better choices are glazed ceramic or
stoneware bowls.

DAIRY DOS *and* DON'TS

. . . .

- Shy away from serving milk, especially to kittens. Their immature digestive systems can't always digest the nutrients in cows' milk. Strange but true: some felines are lactose intolerant.

- Go easy on cheese treats. Cheese is a great calcium source, but too much can cause gas or diarrhea.

- A tablespoon of plain low-fat yogurt once a day is a healthy treat that provides calcium, a dose of "good" bacteria, and some extra liquid (yogurt is mostly water).

Most cats don't care for sweets, but if your kitty begs for a bite of chocolate chip cookie or brownie, resist the temptation to share. Chocolate contains theobromine, a stimulant related to caffeine that can cause a dangerous reaction in cats.

Weigh your cat once a month using the same scale. Record his weight to the exact ounce on a notepad near his food container. A weight gain of one pound on an adult cat over a month's time is your signal to cut back on the serving size and step up the exercise time. Two extra pounds on a cat is like 10 to 20 pounds on a person.

TERRIFIC TIP

For a cat who maintains healthy weight but likes to nibble all day, consider an automatic feeder that dispenses a specified daily portion of dry food. Think of it as cruise control for feline cuisine.

Help a fat feline to lose a few pounds by adding more dietary fiber to his meals with a tablespoon of plain canned pumpkin, a teaspoon of wheat bran, or a half-teaspoon of Metamucil. Fiber improves digestion and helps lessen the chance of constipation while making the cat feel fuller and less inclined to look for more food.

Sprinkle a teaspoon of kelp powder on your cat's food. Or try one standardized capsule of lecithin mixed with her food. Both help to speed your cat's metabolism and break down fats.

Limit your flabby tabby to a 20-minute mealtime.
Remove his dish when the time limit is reached. Leftovers are a clue that you are feeding him too much.

TERRIFIC TIP

Provide finicky eaters with a variety of textures in food. The more pungent the smell of canned food, the greater the appeal.

If you own a fat cat and a slender cat (or a cat and a dog who steals cat food!), you might try putting food in a small dog crate with an opening that will admit only the slimmer feline. You can also install an electronic pet door to a closed-off chow area and outfit only the slender cat with the magnetic collar that gives access.

NUTRITIONAL THERAPY

....

Although manufacturers of commercial cat food are constantly improving and fortifying chow, cats don't always get the right amount of necessary vitamins and minerals. You can put the shine back in your cat's coat, fend off itchy skin, or assist muscle and joint function with supplements. Always discuss your cat's specific supplement needs with your veterinarian.

Here are some popular choices that can keep your cat in optimal health:

Acidophilus. This "good" bacterium detoxifies and fortifies the digestive tract and aids in the absorption of nutrients. Count on this supplement to treat diarrhea, gas, bad breath, and foul-smelling feces.

Amino acids. These are the building blocks of protein that enhance hormone production, maintain healthy muscles and tissues, and keep the metabolism in harmony.

Antioxidants. **Think ACES: vitamins A, C, and E, plus the mineral selenium. Antioxidants help to fend off environmental toxins, lessen the risk for developing certain cancers, and bolster the immune system.**

B-vitamin complex. **Many cats come up short in the B vitamins, which are used to treat stress and cancer. In addition, B vitamins, specifically biotin and folic acid, provide energy, boost the immune system, and help to promote a healthy coat.**

Biotin. **This multi-benefit supplement aids in cellular growth, digestion, muscle formation, and skin repair.**

Brewer's yeast. **This natural source of quality protein, trace minerals, salts, and B-complex vitamins also helps to repel fleas.**

Calcium, magnesium, phosphorus, and zinc. **These minerals work together to keep your cat's nervous system functioning at its best. They also fortify his teeth and bones.**

continued

Cleansers and detoxifiers. **Chlorophyll, algae, barley, wheatgrass, spinach, broccoli, and kelp bolster the immune system and cleanse the blood. These are ideal supplements for aging cats and for those recovering from cancer or surgery.**

Glucosamine and chondroitin. **These supplements help to combat arthritis. They reduce joint swelling, improve circulation, and promote production of synovial fluid to lubricate the joints.**

Omega-3 fatty acids. **This type of fatty acid is helpful for cats with itchy skin caused by allergies.**

Omega-6 fatty acids. **This type of fatty acid helps to restore shine to a dull coat and assists cell development in the brain and immune system.**

Vitamin E. **This vitamin is helpful for arthritis, allergies, skin problems, and heart conditions.**

Keep supplements fresh by storing them in airtight containers. Make sure that you follow label directions. Never exceed the recommended daily amount, because you can potentially harm your cat or worsen a condition.

Hands-on Health & Pampering

HAPPY CAT • HAPPY YOU

Chapter Seven

HOW'S YOUR BEDSIDE MANNER? WHEN IT COMES TO YOUR CAT'S HEALTH, WHAT YOU DO at home in terms of preventive care matters. Shield your cat from disease and injury by taking a hands-on approach. Many problems can be treated more successfully if they're discovered early.

Take on the persona of a feline Florence Nightingale and be on the lookout for any changes in your cat's attitude or appearance. What you discover could save his life, and pampering with a purpose enhances a close connection with your cat chum.

Give your cat a thorough head-to-tail checkup weekly. Just stop short of sticking a tongue depressor into her mouth and asking her to say "aaaahhhh." Devote a hands-on petting session to scrutinize your cat's entire body, looking for lumps, bumps, sore spots, or changes in fur and skin. Don't forget to check her eyes, ears, and mouth. Your observations may help to catch a medical problem in its early stages.

TERRIFIC TIP

Flossing is a good habit to keep your teeth purr-ly white and your gums pink and healthy. However, never leave discarded dental floss in an uncovered wastebasket. A curious cat could ingest it and possibly choke to death.

ME-OW! FIRST-AID KIT

Be ready for any cat-astrophe by keeping a feline first-aid kit on hand. You can dole out the dough for a commercially produced one, but it's easy to create your own. Keep it near a good first-aid book, and make sure that your veterinarian's phone number is readily at hand, along with the address and phone number of the nearest emergency clinic and poison hotline number.

Here's a rundown of must-have items:

- Triple-antibiotic ointment
- Hydrogen peroxide
- Hydrocortisone cream
- Antiseptic wipes
- Bandages and gauze squares
- Stretchy vet wrap
- Cloth tape
- Bandage scissors
- Styptic powder or pencil
- Cotton balls
- Cotton-tipped swabs
- Oral syringe
- Latex gloves
- Cold pack
- Lubricating jelly
- Tweezers
- Metal or digital thermometer

DON'T BE *a* PILL

Pill time — ugh. I'm not sure who dreads this occasion most — you or your cat. Sometimes you can disguise the pill's yucky flavor by cutting it in half with a pill cutter and tucking each piece inside a tiny ball of cream cheese or a bit of cooked fish. Follow this with another treat to make sure that the medicine went down.

If your cat keeps spitting out the pill, however, try Plan B: Open his jaws wide by placing the palm of one hand over the top of his head and applying light pressure with your thumb and forefinger on each side of his mouth. Use your other hand to gently but firmly lower his chin and pop the pill as far back as possible.

Hold his jaws closed with one hand and massage his throat with the other hand to induce swallowing. Try blowing a quick breath of air into his face. When he blinks, he also swallows. Follow up with a treat — both as a reward and to make sure that the pill goes down properly.

When dispensing liquid medicine, tilt your cat's head slightly to one side. Place a plastic dropper — don't use a glass one in case your cat bites down on it — in the side of the cat's mouth at the cheek pouch. Deliver the liquid in one quick squirt and gently hold the jaws shut for a few seconds until you're sure he's swallowed it.

Two more options for cats who are hard to medicate: a pet piller or a transdermal gel. The former is a device that allows you to pop a pill right down your cat's throat with less fuss (and reduces your chance of being bitten), while the latter is an ointment that can be applied to the skin (usually on the ears) where it is absorbed directly into the bloodstream. Ask your veterinarian about these options.

One last tip: If your cat resists your attempts, try again after wrapping him in a towel to hold him still and keep him from scratching you.

WORD *of* WARNING

. . . .

Never give your cat aspirin. Ditto for acetamin-ophen. Her physiology can't tolerate it. A single dose of either can kill a cat.

Monthly household budgets include money for mortgages, car loans, groceries, and health insurance premiums. But many cat lovers — in fact, about 97 percent of us — overlook a potential money-draining item in the household budget: medical expenses for our feline chums. Plan ahead by obtaining pet health insurance.

Premiums vary among companies as well as among cats. Typically, premiums are less expensive for kittens than for senior cats and for healthy cats than for those with diagnosed conditions, such as allergies or cancer. In most cases, the insurance covers 70 to 90 percent of expenses, and some policies include wellness plans.

TERRIFIC TIP

Outfit your cat with a breakaway collar so that she doesn't strangle if it gets caught on something.

Choose your veterinarian wisely. **Word of mouth is a terrific way to locate a skillful veterinarian. Ask responsible pet-caring neighbors, friends, and coworkers for recommendations. You can also contact the American Animal Hospital Association (AAHA) for help. This professional organization promotes standards for pet care and maintains a membership of more than 12,000 licensed veterinarians. Call AAHA's toll-free number at 800-252-2242 or visit the Web site (*www.aahanet.org*) for assistance.**

TAKE *a* TOUR

. . . .

If you're looking for a new veterinarian, ask if you can tour the clinic without your cat before booking your first appointment. High-quality clinics will gladly guide you through their facilities and answer your questions. Look for cleanliness in the waiting room, exam rooms, labs, and boarding areas. Having separate cat and dog waiting areas is a big plus; better yet, many clinics these days cater specifically to cats.

Find out whether the clinic has evening and weekend hours, and ask what you should do in case of an after-hours emergency. You might also inquire about specialties that the veterinary staff may have and whether they take continuing education classes.

If your cat can sniff out a potential vet visit the second you make the appointment, outfox him by shutting him in a small room with few hiding places *before* you take out the carrier. Be calm and speak in reassuring tones when you're ready to round him up because felines are masters at reading our moods — especially when we are stressed or in a hurry. Give yourself plenty of time to ease him into the carrier.

For cats who fight being contained, select a carrier that opens from the top. Then carefully pick up your cat by the scruff of his neck with his legs dangling and guide his hind legs down into the carrier. Gently ease him into the carrier and shut the door.

If you have the kind of carrier that opens from the front, try tipping it so that the door is on top. Once you've put him inside, lower the carrier to the floor slowly, giving your cat a chance to reposition himself.

COOL CATS

. . . .

Go easy on exercise for your cat during humid summer days, especially if she has a short, pushed-in face like a Ragdoll or Persian. These breeds have more difficulty breathing in hot, humid weather.

If your cat does become overheated, gently sponge her paws with a cool (not cold) wet washcloth to lower her core body temperature. Contact your vet if she shows these signs of heat stroke: heavy panting, glazed eyes, vomiting, purple tongue.

WINTER WARINESS

....

Chances are slim that your cat will be begging to go outdoors during cold, snowy days, but if she does escape outside, wash her paws with a dampened towel once you've retrieved her. Chemical salts thrown on sidewalks to melt ice can irritate her foot-pads and can be poisonous if she licks her paws.

TERRIFIC TIP

Always check your washer, dryer, and even your dishwasher before closing the door. Some curious felines like to find cozy, dark places to nap or hide.

POST THIS NUMBER

....

Put this important phone number in a highly visible place: 888-426-4435. This is the toll-free number for the ASPCA's Animal Poison Control Center. Forty veterinary professionals are available day and night for advice. A consultation fee is charged to your credit card, but it is well worth it considering the prompt and knowledgeable attention the center provides.

DENTAL DETAILS

Take care of your cat's teeth and make brushing a bonding time. Praise your cat as you act as her at-home dental hygienist.

For cats not accustomed to having fingers poked inside their mouths, build up trust by dipping your finger into beef bouillon and then rubbing your finger gently over her teeth.

Once your cat is used to the above routine, put gauze over your finger and gently scrub her teeth in a circular motion. Then introduce a nubbed pet thimble or soft toothbrush designed for cats to massage gums and remove plaque buildup.

Choose cat-pleasing toothpaste; it comes in chicken, beef, and liver flavors. Make sure that it contains chlorhexidine, which controls bacteria and fights gum infections.

Gently lift your cat's lip and clean his outside upper teeth, where you're likely to find tartar. Work on one side of your cat's mouth at a time. Pay attention to the crevices where gums and teeth meet.

Schedule a yearly professional cleaning to get rid of stubborn tartar and repair tooth damage. Your cat deserves to sport a fresh, clean smile.

Note: Do NOT use human toothpaste! Not only do cats hate that minty fresh taste, but human products aren't always good for our pets.

Keep your cat's brush within easy reach — for example, next to your recliner in your living room — so that you can groom your cat while you watch your favorite television show. I keep a brush and comb near my balcony door because my two cats love being groomed while we enjoy the morning air and sunshine.

Choose a grooming time when your cat is relaxed and feeling receptive to attention. If possible, set aside five minutes a day to brush your cat. A longhaired cat needs daily brushing to avoid developing mats and tangles.

IT'S SHOCKING!

....

Dry winter air in our homes can cause sparks when we go to pet our cats, and that's no fun at all. Stop the static by using a humidifier — or two, depending on the square footage — in your home.

You can also apply a cat-safe conditioning rinse that rubs into the coat or a spray to maintain some moisture in the coat. Ask at pet supply stores or find a groomer who sells pet products.

Even though cats regularly hone their claws to keep them long and sharp, talon-type nails are definitely not in fashion in the cat world. Regularly clipping your cat's claws is a good idea. Overly sharp claws can snag on carpets and upholstery, potentially causing injuries or infections when the cat yanks free (not to mention rips and snags in the carpet and furniture). There is also an increased risk of injury to children, visitors, and other pets — a cat scratch can be very painful.

NAIL-TRIMMING BASICS

....

Make your "pet-icure" sessions positive and pleasant experiences. Start by gently touching and massaging your cat's feet and immediately giving her a yummy treat as a reward. This accustoms her to having her paws handled and reduces her anxiety when you clip her nails. If you take your time and move quietly and calmly, you should be able to follow these steps toward good grooming:

- Let your cat sniff and investigate the nail trimmer, and offer her a treat.

- Position your cat so that she is in your lap with her back to you.

- Holding one paw, lightly press her toe pads one at a time to extend the claws.

- Quickly snip off the tip of the claw and release the pad.

- If your cat is struggling, trim one paw (or even just one or two claws at first), followed by a treat, and end that session. Do another paw the next day.

- If necessary, conduct the nail trimmings inside a bathroom with the door closed to prevent your cat from escaping.

- When the nail trimming is done, open the door and allow your cat to walk out on her own. Count a few seconds before you depart so that she realizes that you are not chasing or pursuing her.

MORE CLIPPING TIPS

Select clippers that are specifically designed for cats. They do a better and safer job than human clippers will.

If your cat has clear nails, trim just before the quick, the part of the nail that contains blood vessels. If your cat has dark nails and you can't see the quick, clip just the tip every two weeks.

Keep a styptic pencil within reach in case you accidentally cut too deeply and cause bleeding. If you're temporarily out of a styptic product, sprinkle cornstarch on the injured paw to stanch blood flow. Call your vet if the bleeding lasts more than a few minutes.

You won't find many cats leaping into the bathtub, though many cats enjoy keeping their humans company while they bathe, and some love to explore a wet tub or shower stall.

Cats are generally fastidious groomers, but occasionally your cat might need your help to maintain her good looks. Opt for a dry bath, using cat shampoo powder. Let the powder stay in your cat's coat for a few minutes to absorb the oil or dirt, and then brush it out.

TERRIFIC TIP

If your fluffy cat has become a mass of mats, consider a professional grooming session to put you back on track with regular brushing.

GIVE YOUR CAT *the* BRUSH-OFF

. . . .

Use the correct brush for your cat's coat:

- Slicker brushes work on any coat.

- Pin brushes are the top pick for longhaired coats.

- Soft bristle brushes work well on shorthaired coats.

Always stroke in the direction of your cat's fur. Going against the grain with the bristles can irritate your cat's skin and make her want to flee the scene when she sees you pulling out the grooming supplies. Circular motions can break hair, so play it straight.

Provide your cat with her own container of kitty grass to snack on indoors. You can sprout a pot of regular lawn-type grass seed in just a few days. Eating grass provides fiber and can help your cat to boot a must-go hairball from her stomach.

YUCK! TRICHOBEZOAR!

....

That's the scientific term for the common hairball. These disgusting clumps form when a cat swallows the hair that is stripped off by his barbed tongue. Often the hair just passes through the digestive system, but if enough of it is swallowed, it is hacked up, usually in the middle of the night in your bedroom.

Longhaired cats are more likely to produce hairballs, so take extra care in brushing them daily. A dose of hairball remedy every couple of days is a good idea, too.

Use two-sided tape to attach plastic self-grooming combs along the lower corner of a wall. Your cat will enjoy rubbing against the plastic bristles for a self-administered back scratch any time he desires.

TERRIFIC TIP

Run your slightly damp hand gently against the direction of your cat's coat. This technique removes dead hairs better than combing and also promotes new hair growth.

Out of the Ordinary
Holidays, Houseguests, and Hitting the Road

Chapter Eight

HAPPY CAT
HAPPY YOU

CHAPTER 8

CATS CRAVE SET ROUTINES, BUT IN THIS HECTIC WORLD IT IS NEARLY IMPOSSIBLE TO STICK TO one. Life happens. Holidays arrive. Houseguests come toting suitcases. You need to travel — sometimes with your cat. A new job or marriage or other circumstance requires you to move.

The only constant in life is change. Here are ways for you and your habit-craving cat to ease into events — both expected and otherwise.

PARTY *of* ONE

....

Some cats are social butterflies and love a party, but others find a crowd of strangers intimidating. Keep your anxious cat in a quiet part of the house during holiday parties. Provide her with the essentials: water and food, a litter box, a comfy bed, her favorite toy, and some soothing music to mute the chatter from your guests.

It's natural to want to spruce up your home with poinsettias, mistletoe, and holly during the ho-ho-ho days of Christmas, but these holiday favorites can be poisonous to your feline. Either display them well out of reach or strike a safe compromise by selecting faux holiday plants so that your curious cat doesn't become sick from nibbling on the leaves of the real plants.

Love the fresh smell of pine from a real Christmas tree? So does your cat. One way to ensure that your cat doesn't decide to become a real tree hugger and scale your tree is to place orange and lemon peels around the base of the tree. Cats detest citrus smells.

TERRIFIC TIP

Keep your tree standing by using strong fishing line and a pair of ceiling hooks to secure it in place. The fishing line is invisible but will prevent a crash due to a climbing kitty.

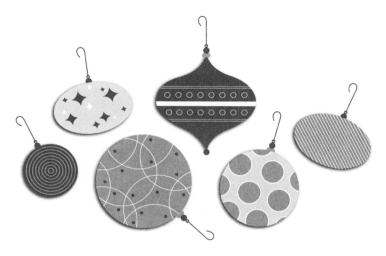

Put lightweight and breakable ornaments high up on your tree to discourage batting and pawing by a curious cat. If your kitty is prone to climbing the tree, you might consider placing family favorites — like that special glass ornament from your great-aunt Jocelyn — in a display case or high on a mantel or table.

Treat your kitty to Christmas or Hanukkah gifts of catnip, toy mice, and cat treats. But don't take out these tempting items until the time is right. Cats are clueless about calendars, and their strong sense of smell may sniff out these gifts before the big day.

TAKE FIVE

....

Pamper your cat and yourself during the some-times stressful holiday season by giving her plenty of reassuring TLC. Treat her to a five-minute therapeutic massage or head-to-tail brushing. Use these mini-sessions to take a few deep, from-the-abdomen breaths while you focus on relaxing and not on what is next on your holiday to-do list.

Don't get so caught up in the holiday spirit that you force your cat to wear a bow around his neck; he can trip or strangle on it. Nix the pair of cloth reindeer antlers, too (let the family dog don goofy holiday headgear instead). If you want to "decorate" the cat, buy her a new collar in cheery holiday colors.

During Thanksgiving and other big feasts, don't share your meal with your cats. Bones can choke animals. Rich gravies and buttery goodies can cause stomachaches. Instead, treat your cats to gourmet cat foods or offer small bits of plain cooked meat to let them share safely in the holiday bounty.

PLANNING AHEAD

....

Where there's a will, there's a way of life for your cat...long after you're gone. The Humane Society of the United States offers a free brochure, "Planning for Your Pet's Future Without You." It outlines steps to take so that your cat will be cared for in a safe, loving environment after you die. You can obtain the brochure by visiting *www.hsus.org*.

Establish a trust that designates someone to care for your cat and provides the finances for lifelong care after you die. You can designate a specific amount to be spent monthly or annually or just leave it up to the executor's discretion. You can also specify that any unused balance of the trust be donated to a favorite animal shelter or other cat charity.

SOOTHING *a* SCAREDY-CAT

....

Halloween can be far from a treat for your cat. Ringing doorbells, kids in costumes shrieking "trick or treat!" and spooky background music are enough to frighten even the mellowest cat. Keep her in a separate room far from the front door. Besides, what's in it for your cat? Felines lack a sweet tooth and no one is handing out tuna treats.

You may love entertaining your friends and hosting houseguests, but your cat may not be so welcoming. When your guests arrive, let them know about your cat's attitude ("Molly doesn't like strangers so just ignore her") and habits ("Max has a tendency to pounce on your ankles as you walk into the kitchen") to minimize surprises during the visit.

Some cats react to visitors by poking their noses into suitcases and staking out a spot on the guest bed. Others may show resentment of the "intruder" by peeing in a visitor's open suitcase. Encourage your guests to keep the bedroom door closed and their personal belongings out of reach.

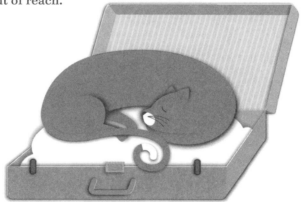

SAYING HELLO

. . . .

If your guests aren't comfortable around cats, tactfully teach them the proper way to meet and greet a feline. The best way is for the guest to sit calmly and extend his index finger for your cat to choose to approach and rub against.

You also need to respect your guest's feelings: some people just don't like cats. If that's the case, make the effort to keep a curious kitty away while you and your friend are visiting. It won't hurt your cat's feelings too much to be shut in a separate room with a new toy for a few hours.

Having visitors is a good opportunity to socialize a shy cat or to reinforce fun tricks that a more confident kitty might like to show off. Let your guests offer tasty treats to create a positive experience for a cat who may be wary of strangers. If your cat is a natural ham, show your visitor how to put him through his paces.

WARNING: TRICKY CATS

. . . .

Post funny notes on brightly colored paper by your front and back doors to remind your guests not to leave the doors open for Houdini cat to slip outside.

My favorite note at one friend's house read: "The real owner of this house is a four-legged escape artist. Please keep the doors closed."

CATS *in* CARS

....

Most cats aren't big fans of traveling, and it's no wonder when their usual destination is the vet's office. If your cat goes into full-scale panic mode whenever he's in the car, try a desensitizing program. Do each of the following steps several times over several days before moving on to the next one.

1. Start by spending 5 to 10 minutes in the car with the engine off. If your cat isn't too nervous to eat, offer a really great treat that you know he's bonkers for. Bring your cat back inside and let him return to his usual routine.

2. Put your cat in the car, offer him that special "it's great to be in the car" treat, and then drive around the block. Bring him home and let him relax.

3. Work your way up to longer trips slowly. Take a couple of drives that equal the distance to the vet's office, but come home instead of taking him into the office.

Your cat may never delight in taking a road trip, but these steps should help him become more comfortable in the car.

LONGER DRIVES

....

Hold off on feeding your cat for a few hours prior to the start of your trip. No need to increase the risk of vomiting caused by motion sickness or worse: an unexpected bout of diarrhea. If your cat does have a tendency to get sick in the car, talk to your vet about medications to reduce nausea.

TERRIFIC TIP

Carry water for your cat, even
on short rides. A quick trip can
sometimes unexpectedly become a long
journey. Also bring some dry food
in an airtight container.

Never leave your cat inside the car in the hot summer — not even for a few minutes. Leaving the windows open a crack is no guarantee against heat-stroke. Your cat can become severely sick or even die.

BUCKLE UP

. . . .

Having a small creature slip under your feet while you're using the pedals is an invitation to disaster. Some manufacturers offer sturdy, partially open cat carriers that permit cats to take in the view without roaming loose in the car.

Check pet supply stores for carriers that feature a quick-release snap that attaches to the vehicle's seat belt. A strong, plastic body, a washable comfort pad, and adjustable nylon carrying straps are also good features.

If you are one of those people who is a magnet for lost animals, store a collapsible carrier in the trunk so that you will always have one handy in case you find a stray kitty wandering the streets. Stash an extra leash and collar, a sealed bag of treats, a collapsible water bowl, and a catnip mouse as well.

Taking your pet with you on trips is growing in popularity, and it's not just dogs who are hitting the road. More and more hotels are putting the welcome mat out for well-behaved pet visitors. Practice proper *pet-iquette* while traveling with your feline mate by abiding by the hotel's pet policy.

TIPS *for* TRAVELING TABBIES

....

- Don't try to sneak your pet into a hotel. Book ahead at a place that accepts animals.

- Take a portable litter box with plenty of fresh litter (and don't forget the scooper) and some disposal bags.

- Pack your cat's favorite blanket or bedding to make her feel more at home in an otherwise strange place.

- Never allow your cat to roam freely in the room while you're out. Keep her feeling cozy inside her carrier with a favorite toy, food and water, a blanket, and a mini litter box.

Check out these Web sites for hotels, motels, and inns all over the United States that accept pets:

> *www.fidofriendly.com*
> *www.petsonthego.com*
> *www.takeyourpet.com*

TERRIFIC TIP

For long road trips, place your cat in a carrier that has space for a small litter box. But bring a smaller carrier, too. That way, you can keep your cat safe in the backup carrier while you're cleaning the litter box.

NO METAL-STUDDED COLLARS

....

Cats are not big fans of flying. The noise of the plane and the scary sights, sounds, and smells of an airport are big feline turnoffs. When you do need to travel with your cat, realize that you may be asked to take your cat out of her carrier and walk through the metal detector with her in your arms. Prevent your feline from fleeing by putting her in a harness and attaching the leash before removing her from the carrier at the security checkpoint.

TIPS *for* AIR TRAVEL

- Book early. Some airlines limit the total number of animals per flight to two or three. Most make pet reservations on a first-come, first-served basis.

- A cat under 15 pounds may be able to ride with you in a carrying case in the passenger section on some airlines. The crate must be able to slide easily under the seat in front of you. Acceptable carriers are 23 inches long by 13 inches wide by 9 inches high, but check with the airline.

- Seek direct flights whenever possible to avoid transfers and delays.

- Always travel on the same flight as your cat.

- Schedule an appointment with your veterinarian no more than 10 days before the scheduled flight to ensure that your feline is fit to fly.

- Take a current photograph of your cat with you. If your cat gets lost in the airport or at the destination, the photo can make the search go much more smoothly.

- Store the leash in your carry-on luggage and not inside the crate. This keeps your cat from accidentally getting caught or strangled, or having the leash get lost.

- Don't put food in the crate. The ride is upsetting for cats and can lead to digestive problems.

- Pack some paper towels in your carry-on bag for cleaning up any messes.

- Make sure that all of your contact information, including your destination, is clearly and permanently fixed to the outside of the travel crate.

PEACE *of* MIND

....

If you're going to be away from home for two or more days and you don't know any cat-savvy neighbors, rely on a professional pet sitter to cater to your cat's daily needs. This is a growing business, so there are bound to be a few pet sitters in your area. For planned trips, it's best to contact and interview a pet sitter a couple of weeks in advance.

For local referrals, contact the National Association of Professional Pet Sitters (NAPPS) at 800-296-PETS or check out their Web site at *www.petsitters.org*. You can also contact Pet Sitters International (PSI) at 336-983-9222 or *www.petsit.com*. The staff at your veterinary clinic or local cat club may also be able to recommend pet sitters in your area.

TERRIFIC TIP

Introduce your pet sitter to a friendly neighbor and have them exchange phone numbers. This way your neighbors are aware of this "stranger" in your house, and the pet sitter has an ally nearby.

HIRING *a* PET SITTER

Here are some things you need to know before hiring a pet sitter:

- Is this person licensed and bonded?

- Does he or she have the necessary training to give medications to your pet?

- How much experience does he or she have?

- Will he or she stay at your home overnight or come to visit once or twice a day (or more)?

Ask for references before you interview anyone. Have the sitter come to meet your cat before you go away. See how your cat reacts. Does she seem relaxed and comfortable with this person?

Once you've hired someone, make sure to leave the following information in a central spot:

- Names (and silly nicknames!), as well as descriptions of each cat in the house

- Location of food (have a backup supply, just in case)

- Daily feeding routine, including limits on treats

- Location and description of any medications

- Instructions for administering medications

- Your itinerary and contact information and the phone number of a friend or neighbor

- The name and phone number of your veterinarian, as well as directions to the animal clinic and instructions for after-hours emergencies

- A list of particular quirks or habits that might be helpful to know: "Emma will meow until you fill the water bowl in the bathroom every morning." "If you can't find Riley, look in the closet in the den."

Develop a network of cat-sitting friends and neighbors for those weekends away or brief business trips. Offer to take care of their cats while they travel. This is also a great job for a responsible neighborhood teenager who loves animals. Having the same person come every time you travel helps your pet to feel more secure in your absence.

"I love my cats because I love my home, and little by little they become its visible soul."

— Jean Cocteau

RESOURCES

....

American Association of Feline
Practitioners
www.aafponline.org

American Humane Association
www.americanhumane.org

American Society for the
Prevention of Cruelty to
Animals
www.aspca.org

Cat Fanciers' Association
www.cfa.org

Delta Society
www.deltasociety.org

Humane Society of the United
States
www.hsus.org

Winn Feline Foundation
www.winnfelinehealth.org

ANIMAL BEHAVIOR

Animal Behavior Network
www.animalbehavior.net

Certified Applied Animal
Behaviorists
*www.certifiedanimalbehaviorist.
com*

International Association of
Animal Behavior Consultants
www.iaabc.org

FINDING LOST PETS

Petfinder
www.petfinder.com

Pets 911
www.pets911.com

PET HEALTH AND NEWS

Animal Radio
www.animalradio.com

ASPCA Poison Control Center
Hotline
888-426-4435
www.aspca.org

Cat Channel
www.catchannel.com

National Association of
Professional Pet Sitters
www.petsitters.org

Pets Best Insurance Services
www.petsbest.com

RENTING WITH PETS

Humane Society of the United
States
www.rentwithpets.org

Pet Life Radio
www.petliferadio.com

Pet Relocation
www.petrelocation.com

Pet Sitters International
www.petsit.com

PET TRAVEL

Fido Friendly magazine
www.fidofriendly.com

Pets on the Go
www.petsonthego.com

Take Your Pet
www.takeyourpet.com

INDEX

OTHER STOREY TITLES
YOU WILL ENJOY

. . . .

The Cat Behavior Answer Book, by **Arden Moore.**
Practical insights into the feline mind — for cat owners
everywhere!
336 pages. Paper. ISBN 978-1-58017-674-3.

Dr. Kidd's Guide to Herbal Cat Care, by **Randy Kidd, DVM, PhD.**
Thorough information on using all-natural herbal remedies to
treat and prevent disease in your favorite feline.
208 pages. Paper. ISBN 978-1-58017-188-5.

Happy Dog, Happy You, by **Arden Moore.**
Gentle humor and inspired advice from a pet expert to
owners and their canine friends.
304 pages. Paper. ISBN 978-1-60342-032-7.

The Kitten Owner's Manual, by **Arden Moore.**
Solutions to all your kitten quandaries, from a cat expert.
208 pages. Paper. ISBN 978-1-58017-387-2.

Real Food for Cats, by **Patti Delmonte.**
Nutritionally balanced, vet-approved, no-fuss recipes
guaranteed to satisfy the cats in your household.
128 pages. Paper. ISBN 978-1-58017-409-1.

These and other books from Storey Publishing are available
wherever quality books are sold or by calling 1-800-441-5700.
Visit us at *www.storey.com*.